M000121333

EMBRACE YOUR RENEWAL

Visit our website at
WWW.ALBAHOUSE.ORG

or call 1-800-343-2522 (ALBA)
and request current catalog

Embrace Your Renewal
A Thought a Day for Lent

HAROLD A. BUETOW, PHD, JD

ST PAULS

Alba
House

Library of Congress Cataloging-in-Publication Data

Buetow, Harold A.
   Embrace your renewal : a thought a day for Lent / Harold A. Buetow.
      p. cm.
   ISBN 0-8189-0959-5
      1. Lent—Prayer-books and devotions—English.   2. Devotional calendars.   I. Title.

   BV85.B77 2004
   242'.34—dc21

                                        2003012037

Produced and designed in the United States of America by the
Fathers and Brothers of the Society of St. Paul,
2187 Victory Boulevard, Staten Island, New York 10314-6683,
as part of their communications apostolate.

ISBN: 0-8189-0959-5

© Copyright 2004 by the Society of St. Paul

Printing Information:

Current Printing - first digit	1	2	3	4	5	6	7	8	9	10

Year of Current Printing - first year shown

2004	2005	2006	2007	2008	2009	2010	2011	2012

I am once again grateful to so many people
for help in the compilation of these thoughts
as to make them impossible to recount.

I am, however, most indebted to
Dr. Rose M. Auteri
Patricia C. Deeley, M.A.
Steven Krogman and
Col. (Ret.) Michael L. Wardinski, Ph.D.

Table of Contents

Biblical Abbreviations

OLD TESTAMENT

Genesis	Gn	Nehemiah	Ne	Baruch	Ba
Exodus	Ex	Tobit	Tb	Ezekiel	Ezk
Leviticus	Lv	Judith	Jdt	Daniel	Dn
Numbers	Nb	Esther	Est	Hosea	Ho
Deuteronomy	Dt	1 Maccabees	1 M	Joel	Jl
Joshua	Jos	2 Maccabees	2 M	Amos	Am
Judges	Jg	Job	Jb	Obadiah	Ob
Ruth	Rt	Psalms	Ps	Jonah	Jon
1 Samuel	1 S	Proverbs	Pr	Micah	Mi
2 Samuel	2 S	Ecclesiastes	Ec	Nahum	Na
1 Kings	1 K	Song of Songs	Sg	Habakkuk	Hab
2 Kings	2 K	Wisdom	Ws	Zephaniah	Zp
1 Chronicles	1 Ch	Sirach	Si	Haggai	Hg
2 Chronicles	2 Ch	Isaiah	Is	Malachi	Ml
Ezra	Ezr	Jeremiah	Jr	Zechariah	Zc
		Lamentations	Lm		

NEW TESTAMENT

Matthew	Mt	Ephesians	Eph	Hebrews	Heb
Mark	Mk	Philippians	Ph	James	Jm
Luke	Lk	Colossians	Col	1 Peter	1 P
John	Jn	1 Thessalonians	1 Th	2 Peter	2 P
Acts	Ac	2 Thessalonians	2 Th	1 John	1 Jn
Romans	Rm	1 Timothy	1 Tm	2 John	2 Jn
1 Corinthians	1 Cor	2 Timothy	2 Tm	3 John	3 Jn
2 Corinthians	2 Cor	Titus	Tt	Jude	Jude
Galatians	Gal	Philemon	Phm	Revelation	Rv

A priest was coming back to his rectory
one evening in the dark, only to be accosted
by a robber who pulled a gun at him and demanded,
"Your money or your life!"
As the priest reached his hand into his coat pocket,
the robber saw his Roman collar and said,
"I see you're a priest. Never mind, you can go."
The priest, surprised at this unexpected
show of piety, tried to reciprocate
by offering the robber
a bar of candy that he remembered
was in his pocket, to which the robber replied,
"No, Father, I don't eat candy during Lent."

Introduction to the Lenten Season

Origins of Lent

Before we begin this season we need to correct such misunderstandings. The word *Lent* comes from the Old English word *lencten* — meaning, literally, the lengthening of the hours of daylight, or "Springtime." It's our springtime of the spirit — a season when, like new life being wrested from the clutch of winter, our opportunities for spiritual flowering and growth joyfully revive.

From the beginning, Lent was established as a time of penance preparing for the celebration of Easter. Initially a three-day observance of strict fast covering the three Great Days of Holy Week, it was later expanded to cover all of Holy Week, and then to three weeks. Originally, the emphasis was exclusively on the pastoral and liturgical preparation of converts for baptism at the Easter Vigil. That emphasis was later virtually overtaken by another tradition, originating in the monasteries of Europe: the imitation of Jesus' days of reflection in the desert. The new converts preparing for baptism who were known to be guilty of serious sin were excluded from the Eucharistic celebration until confession on Holy Thursday; other preparing converts could attend only the first part of the Mass, the Mass of the catechumens, until baptism at the Easter Vigil. This broke down when the now numerous converts had children and the baptism of their infants replaced adult baptism as the general practice of the

Church. In 325 A.D., the Council of Nicaea regulated the practice of forty days of Lenten penance from Ash Wednesday until Easter Sunday.

The number forty occurs frequently in Scripture. After Moses had made the covenant with God on Mount Sinai and then discovered the Jewish people guilty of idolatry, he spent forty days of fasting on the mountain before he again took up his leadership role. After that, the Jews wandered in the desert for forty years, often hungry and thirsty. The great prophet Elijah fasted for forty days in the desert. God directed Jonah to give the populace of Nineveh forty days to repent before catastrophe would strike. In the New Testament, Jesus prepared for his public ministry with a period of forty days of fasting in the desert. The risen Jesus spent forty days with the Apostles before his ascension into heaven.

Scholars don't have a definitive answer to whether the number forty was used literally or figuratively in Scripture. Nor can they say for sure what the symbolic meaning of the number may have been. But it's often speculated that the ancients' interest in the symbolism of numbers played a part. Sometimes numbers had significance because of the multiple. For example, the number four was significant to those in biblical times who considered it a symbol of the four directions of the winds; multiplied by ten — the number of fingers on both hands — the number may have taken on significance in itself.

The severity of the Lenten penance was greatly mitigated by Pope Paul VI in 1966. He did, however, urge an increase in acts of piety such as attending Mass, making visits to the Blessed Sacrament, being more prayerful, and donating money to charitable causes. And, after the Second Vatican Council in 1965, the Church got back to the baptismal emphasis, with the renewal of the Rite of Christian Initiation for Adults.

The readings for the Lenten weekday Masses for the first three weeks take their gospel reading from Sts. Matthew, Mark, and Luke, with emphasis on the cures and works of Jesus. From the fourth week on, gospel passages are from St. John, centering on the person of the Lord and fitting for those about to commit themselves to him.

Why Lent?

All religions see the need for mortification. The shamans among the Tungus of Siberia fast and train themselves to control spirits. The Pueblo Indians of the southwestern United States fast before major ceremonies. In a widespread religious practice going back to the ancients, fasting prepared people, especially priests and priestesses, to approach the deities. With the healing cult of the god Asclepius in the Hellenistic mystery religions, divine teachings were often revealed only after a fast that required total devotion. Judaism developed many customs of fasting. Buddhist monks fast on certain days. Hindu *sadhus* (holy men) are admired for their frequent personal fasts. The month of Ramadan in Islam is observed as a period of penitence and total fasting from dawn to dusk. Mahatma Gandhi, among others, used fasting for social and political purposes.

Lent is the season that calls us to turn our hearts to God. "Jesus' call to conversion and penance, like that of the prophets before him, does not aim first at outward works, sackcloth and ashes, fasting and mortification, but at the conversion of heart, interior conversion" (*Catechism of the Catholic Church*, #430). It's not just negative, but positive, too, hopefully providing an opportunity to see ourselves correctly. A woman complained to a visiting friend that her neighbor was a poor housekeeper. "You should see how dirty her children are — and her house! It's almost a disgrace to be living in the same neighborhood. Take a look at those clothes she has hanging on her line. See the black streaks in the sheets and towels?" The friend walked up to the window and said, "I think the clothes are quite clean, my dear. The streaks are on your window."

For the Christian, Lent means an opportunity to banish ignorance, to deaden lust, to enrich the poor, to defend children, to make decent medical care as globally ubiquitous as Coca-Cola, and to end many world catastrophes. Mortification guides our imagination and memory by keeping away useless or harmful thoughts, and it may also help control the tongue from useless and frivolous conversations or gossip.

Motivation

We can't make heaven and hell the sole motivation for Lent, any more than we can for our lives. An old Irish tale tells of Paddy walking along a country road and meeting an angel. The angel had a firebrand in one hand and a pail of water in the other. In answer to Paddy's question about the baggage, the angel answered, "With the pail of water I'm going to put out the fires of hell, and with the firebrand I'm going to set fire to all the mansions of heaven. Then we'll see whose life motivations are proper!"

A prime Lenten motivation is the health of our spiritual life. That isn't a quick sprint to a well-marked finish line, but a marathon, an arduous lifelong journey into an ever-widening horizon. To sustain ourselves, even after we have some assurance that we're on the right road, requires that along the way we continually find what metaphorically might be termed "Elijah's jug" (1 K 17:1-8). The jar of flour and the jug of oil of the widow who fed Elijah never went empty. God promises to provide for those who are walking the long road toward the divine mountain.

Lenten Themes

Many Lenten themes can be found in the season's liturgies. In the Prefaces of the Masses, for example, we're presented with the spiritual meaning of Lent (that it's a joyful season in which we renew our mind and heart to prepare to celebrate the paschal mystery, a spirit of loving reverence for our heavenly Father and of willing service to our neighbor); the spirit of penance (to purify our hearts, to control our desires, and so to serve God in freedom; how to live in this passing world with our heart set on the world that will never end); the fruits of self-denial (that it masters our sinfulness and conquers our pride); the reward of fasting (that it corrects our faults, raises our minds to God, helps us to grow in holiness, and offers us the reward of everlasting life). Lent can rid us of the hidden corruption of evil; Lent helps us prepare to share Jesus' paschal meal in purity of heart; Lent gives us a realization of the meaning of our baptism; Lent helps us understand the power of the cross; Lent provides a realization of Jesus' life-giving death and glorious resurrection; and it's a preparation for the great event of our redemption.

Random selections from the opening prayers of weekday Lenten Masses reveal similar themes. Protect us in our struggle against evil. Bring us the blessing of God's forgiveness and the gift of His light. Help us to resist temptation by our Lenten works of charity and penance. Prepare us to celebrate the death and resurrection of Christ our Savior. May our Lenten penance give God glory (seldom heard as a motivation for anything these days). That our sacrifice of praise and reconciliation free us from sin and enable us to give God loving service. That by the good works God inspires we may be helped to discipline our bodies and be renewed in spirit. Help us to know what is right and be eager to do God's will.

The Lenten Masses pray also that we become a people who worship God in spirit and truth. Teach us to find new life through penance. Keep us from sin, and help us live by God's commandment of love. Teach us to live good lives. Send the Holy Spirit to make us strong in faith and active in good works. May our acts of penance bring us God's forgiveness, open our hearts to our heavenly Father's love, and prepare us for the coming feast of the resurrection. Help us to live the love these practices proclaim.

These prayers ask God to bring us together in unity and peace. Keep us faithful to the gospel of Christ; give us the grace to rise above our human weakness. Please, God, make this Lenten observance of the suffering, death, and resurrection of Christ bring us to the full joy of Easter. May we, God's church, grow in His life and continue to receive His help on earth. May our Lenten observance prepare us to embrace the paschal mystery and to proclaim the Lord's salvation with joyful praise. May the love within us be seen in what we do and lead us to the joy of Easter. Help us to pass from our old life of sin to the new life of grace. May we offer God hearts purified by bodily penance. Help us to do God's will that His church may grow and become more faithful in His service. Enlighten our minds and sanctify our hearts. Help us to remain faithful to a holy way of life, and guide us to the inheritance God has promised. May we come to share in the glory of the Lord's resurrection.

Holy Mother the Church repeats many times during Lent, especially the theme of reconciliation and forgiveness. For example, Ash Wednesday begins Lent with the Lord's call to "return to me with your whole heart." On the Saturday after that, Jesus assures us that he hasn't come to invite the self-righteous to a change of heart, but sinners. Tuesday of the First Week of Lent gives us the Lord's Prayer with its postscript that if we forgive the faults of others, our heavenly Father will forgive us ours. On Friday of that same week we're told to go first to be reconciled with anyone who has anything against us, and then come and offer our gift. The next day, Jesus gives his command to love our enemies, pray for our persecutors. On Monday of the Second Week we hear that if we pardon we shall be pardoned. On that Saturday, the gospel tells us about the father's welcoming home his prodigal son. And so on — we get the point!

Encouragement

Through all our Lenten sacrifices and mortifications, we're from time to time given needed encouragement on the uses of adversity. Ten-year-old Sarah was born with a muscle missing in her foot and wore a brace all the time. One beautiful spring day she came home to her mother and father to tell them that she had competed in "field day" — a day when they have races and other competitive events. Before her parents could get a word out, she said, "Mommy and Daddy, I won two of the races!" They couldn't believe it. Then Sarah said, "I had an advantage." They thought she may have been given a head start. But again before they could say anything, Sarah added, "I didn't get a head start: My advantage was that I had to try harder!"

If we practice the mortifications of Lent seriously, we shall perhaps sometimes experience the discouragement of the composer Anton Bruckner. He began writing his Fifth Symphony only weeks after telling a friend that his life had "lost all its joy and pleasure — it has been vain and for nothing." Yet what pours forth from the score of this symphony is a sense of triumph over adversity. Melancholy string themes and tragic full-orchestra choral passages give way to sumptuous brass chorales, and Bruckner's final word is an emphatic, bright-hued statement of the chorale.

It's easy to get discouraged when things are going bad. But we shouldn't lose heart, because God is at work in our lives, even in the midst of pain and suffering. For all the negative things we may have to say about Lent and life, God has a positive answer. You say, "It's impossible"; God says: "All things are possible" (Lk

18:27). You say, "I'm too tired"; God says, "I will give you rest" (Mt 11:28). You say, "Nobody really loves me"; God says, "I love you" (Jn 3:16). You say, "I can't go on"; God says, "My grace is enough" (2 Cor 12:9). You say, "I can't figure things out"; God says, "I will direct your steps" (Pr 3:5f.). You say, "I can't do it"; God says He gives strength for everything (Ph 4:13). You say, "It's not worth it"; God says He makes all things work together (Rm 8:28). You say, "I can't forgive myself"; God says He forgives you (1 Jn 1:9; Rm 8:1). You say, "I can't manage"; God says, "I will supply all your needs" (Ph 4:19). You say, "I'm afraid"; God says He has given us a spirit that is strong, loving, and wise (2 Tm 1:7). You say, "I'm always worried and frustrated"; God says that we're to cast all our cares on Him (1 P 5:7). You say, "I don't have enough faith"; God says He has given everyone a measure of faith (Rm 12:3). You say, "I'm not smart enough"; God says He has given you wisdom (1 Cor 1:30). You say, "I feel all alone"; God says, "I will never desert you, nor will I forsake you" (Heb 13:5).

Because Lent gives opportunities particularly in the three areas of fasting, giving (of self: time, talent, and treasure), and prayer, we include a few introductory words about each.

FASTING

Fasting isn't the same as dieting. The purpose of dieting is to improve the health and beauty of our bodies. The purpose of fasting is to turn our attention to God, other people, and ourselves. Dieting means the regulation of food intake as a health measure — as in low-calorie, low-fat, or low-sodium foods. Fasting as we mean it in religion is to abstain from food voluntarily for a time and to eat sparingly as a spiritual exercise. Though both dieting and fasting can have physical benefits, only fasting gives spiritual ones.

Like mortification in general, the practice of limiting the amounts and kinds of our food and drink are forms of penance common to all great religions. People fast partly in order to overcome an indulgent spirit which seeks comfort and pleasure above all else. Thomas Merton wrote that the desires for food, drink, sex, and pleasure are like little children — insistent, constantly clamoring for attention. A real fast — the kind which truly honors God — is the kind of self-denial which, in the prophet Isaiah's words, results in deeds of justice and compassion, in freeing the oppressed, in sharing one's bread with the hungry.

Prosperous countries like the United States can perhaps benefit most from both dieting and fasting. With the exception of the population of a few Pacific islands, our citizens are the heaviest people in the history of the world — a nation of fat behinds and paunchy stomachs. Early in the Twentieth Century, the principal causes of death and disability in the United States were infectious diseases. Today, many health problems are related to the overconsumption of calories. Overeating unsettles metabolism and increases the likelihood of chronic diseases like hypertension, coronary heart disease, some cancers, stroke, diabetes, and others.

In the year 2000, United States inhabitants spent $110 billion on "fast food": more than on higher education, personal computers, software, or new cars — the main reasons being inexpensiveness and convenience. One writer said that McDonald's golden arches are better known around the world than the Christian cross. Fast food is so processed and denatured that it's necessary to manufacture much of the taste and aroma, a technological feat that's performed in a series of large chemical plants off the New Jersey Turnpike.

Why Fast?

Pope St. Leo the Great wrote: "There is a great difference... between the pleasures of the body and those of the heart.... In carnal pleasures the appetite causes satiety and satiety generates dissatisfaction. In spiritual pleasures, on the other hand, when the appetite gives birth to satiety, satiety then gives birth to greater appetite. Spiritual delights increase the extent of desire in the mind even when they satisfy the appetite for them. The more one recognizes the taste of such things, the more one recognizes what it is that one loves so strongly."

There's something in many of us that seeks a reward of virtue. Napoleon is reported to have said, "men are led by such baubles." George Patton said in 1918, "I'd rather be a second lieutenant with a DSC (Distinguished Service Cross) than a general without it." In life, as well as in the military, people like baubles: ribbons, medals, certificates, trinkets. But maturity has to set that straight.

Jenny, a bright young teenager on the brink of maturity, was shopping with her mother when she spotted a beautiful imitation pearl necklace. She asked her mother if she could have it. Her mother said, "Well, it's a pretty necklace, but it costs a lot of money." Seeing how badly Jenny wanted this necklace, she added, "I'll tell you what. I'll buy the necklace for you and when we get back home we can make a list of chores you can do to pay for it. Okay?"

Jenny eagerly agreed. She worked on her chores every day until she finally paid off the necklace. She loved those imitation pearls so much that she wore them everywhere, even to bed.

Jenny's father observed how much she loved her necklace and would from time to time ask her if she would be willing to give it to him. Each time she responded "Oh, Daddy, not my pearl necklace. I love you very much, but I can't give you my necklace. But you can have my very favorite CD album — or you can have my very favorite…" to which her dad interrupted, "No, that's OK" and brushed her face with a tender kiss.

Then one day, expecting her dad to ask her for her pearl necklace again, with trembling lips she greeted him with "Here, Daddy!" and held out her beloved necklace. She knuckled the tears from her eyes.

With one hand her father accepted the imitation pearls and with the other he silently pulled a blue velvet box from his pocket and handed it to her. When Jenny opened the box, her eyes went wide with joy. Nestled in the blue velvet inside was a string of genuine pearls, luminescent with beauty. Her father had been keeping them all along, patiently waiting for Jenny to give up the fake, cheap stuff so he could give her the real thing.

Our heavenly Father is waiting for us to surrender the cheap stuff that our flesh so loves, so that He can replace it with the beautiful and eternal treasures of the spirit. Fasting corrects our faults, raises our minds to God, helps us to grow in holiness, and offers us the reward of everlasting life. As Isaiah said (58:4), "Would that today you might fast so as to make your voice heard on high!" There are, in fact, many other good reasons for fasting. One is that voluntarily abstaining from food as well as other legitimate pleasures makes us less attached to things, more in control of our lives. Another is that, by giving things up, we might appreciate them the more: One who has to leave home for a while comes to an enhanced appreciation of home.

How to Fast

There are many ways to fast. The Pharisees of Jesus' time used fasting for display — they whitened their faces and wore old clothes so people would know they were fasting and, they hoped, admire them. Jesus advised, however, "When you fast, you are not to look glum as the hypocrites do" (Mt 6:16).

The Church asks all of us to abide by certain (really rather minimal) restrictions with regard to amounts of food and the abstention from meat. We can add others: skipping a meal occasionally, and donating the money we would have spent on it to the poor. Or at times — perhaps on a Friday here or there — we can engage in a "black fast," consuming only bread and water for the entire day.

Perhaps we can move imaginatively into the experience of Jesus in the desert and confront our demons — those finite goods that most threaten to take the place of God in our life: power, money, esteem, sex, pleasure. St. Athanasius wrote: "Devils take great delight in fullness, and drunkenness, and bodily comfort. Fasting possesses great power and it works glorious things.... To fast is to banquet with angels."

When to Fast

One of the most frequently quoted texts of the Old Testament is the passage that begins, "There is an appointed time for everything..." (Ec 3:1). The Christian calendar prescribes days and seasons of feasting and fasting. They interact: fasting makes feasting more joyous and feasting demands fasting to make it intelligible. For fasting, Lent is a very good time. Catholic sections of the world have gotten it right: they celebrate the joyful anticipation of Lenten fasting. The German *fastnacht, mardi gras* in the French tradition, and *carnivale* in the Italian custom are all celebrations in anticipation of the beginning of the Lenten season of fasting.

Some of John the Baptist's disciples and the Pharisees were accustomed to fast, and Jesus' disciples were not. When asked about this, Jesus used an analogy that people at that time would have understood well: a comparison of himself to a bridegroom, a figure John the Baptist had used (Jn 3:29). He was comparing his disciples to the "sons of the nuptial couch," a picturesque Semitic term for the closest friends of the bridal couple who by their talk and songs saw to it that the wedding party went off with panache. The bridegroom, like most people of that time, worked hard and didn't go away on a honeymoon; he stayed home amid continued rejoicing that lasted for a week. Wedding guests, who came and went during the week, were exempt from the rules of fasting. It was supposed to be the happiest week in anyone's life. Fasting will be appropriate, Jesus says, when the wedding party of his physical presence is over.

ALMSGIVING — OR SELF-GIVING, OR WORKS OF MERCY

The Paradoxes of Almsgiving

Almsgiving is full of paradoxes. For one, Jesus told us that there's more happiness in giving than in receiving (Ac 20:35). The inclination to give is rooted in the depths of the human heart. People who respond to the impulse to give themselves to others without expecting anything in return experience a profound interior satisfaction. Giving to the needy not only from our abundance, but sacrificing something more, fosters the kind of self-denial that's essential to authentic Christian living.

Especially during Lent, we're called to follow in the footsteps of Jesus who, in perfect obedience to the heavenly Father's will, emptied himself (Ph 2:6ff.). The Son of God loved us first, while we were yet sinners (Rm 5:8), asking nothing in return. Even though at times it isn't the Christian command of love which motivates our efforts to help others, but an innate sense of compassion, everyone who helps those in need enjoys God's favor. In the Acts of the Apostles we read of a convert named Tabitha whose life was marked by constant good deeds. When she died, she was rewarded by St. Peter raising her back to life

(Ac 9:36ff.). We read also of a Roman centurion, Cornelius, who secured eternal life because of his "habit of giving generously" (Ac 10:2ff.).

We can't seek the true good of our fellow human beings — deeply, lastingly — without embodying the charity of Jesus. That's the kind of love given by missionaries risking their lives in different parts of the world, by those who have embraced a vocation to the priesthood or the religious life, by parents who devote themselves to their children, and by the growing number of volunteers who readily devote themselves to helping the poor, the elderly, the sick, and others in need.

At the same time, paradoxically, the spirit of our world encourages our desire to possess and drives us to satisfy our own interests. The words of St. Paul to Timothy still remain relevant: "The love of money is the root of all evil" (1 Tm 6:10). And the exploitation of others, indifference toward others' suffering, and the violation of basic rules of morality are a few of the fruits of the hunger for gain.

Equally paradoxically, all over the world the gulf between rich and poor seems to be widening. We enter a cycle of envy and guilt: as it gets tougher to make ends meet, we sometimes feel resentful or jealous of others who have more than we; at the same time, when we see pictures of starving children we feel guilty about what we have.

Lent is a good time to break out of this cycle. We come to recognize that our most precious commodities — health, friendship, love, the beauty of creation — are pure gifts from God. Gratitude for what we have prompts us to do something for those in need — not out of guilt, but out of compassion. This compassion involves giving not only from our surplus, but also from our substance.

There's at least one other paradox to poverty. Idealistic Christianity wants its members to live humbly. But some Germanic pagans once responded to a shoeless missionary bishop by saying: "How can we believe you are a messenger of the most high God, who is glorious and filled with riches, whereas you're so poor that you can't afford shoes?"

In some ways, giving has become a fad. Actors and actresses, famous sports figures, and politicians all participate in benefit galas; airlines collect change from their passengers for orphans; and companies sponsor and plaster their logos on fund-raising materials. In many cases, giving seems to promise donors glory and greatness if they ignore Jesus' instructions not to let their left hand know what their right hand is doing.

Why Give?

Though a hardened member of a secular society may say to the poor, or homeless, or frightened, or sick, "Sorry, but that's your problem," no member of Jesus' Church can say that to any member of the human race, all of whom we're taught to see as a brother or sister. Our Church isn't a club, just a collectivity of like-minded people. In the image proposed by St. Paul (Rm 12:4f., etc.), it's a living body, composed of thousands of interdependent organs and cells, and ensouled by Jesus Christ.

Jesus identified with the poor, and God Himself is present in them. Those who love God welcome the poor. Though the poor may be hard to find, they exist worldwide. Despite rosy promises to the poor — the end of welfare as we know it, rising economic tides lifting everybody's boats — they're not doing very well at all. They're not in the same neighborhoods or the same schools as the well-to-do. They're not on television, except for crime scenes. They've vanished from the country's political discussion. For all its riches, the United States now has a greater percentage of its citizens in prison or on the streets, and more neglected children, than any other advanced nation.

A recent researcher on poverty spent the better part of two

years trying to survive on jobs in the United States that paid the minimum wage. She worked in jobs that included waitress, hotel maid, cleaning woman, nursing-home aide, and sales clerk. In one place she lived in a trailer park, and in another place briefly in a hideous motel room that was pretty much open to anyone's view or to anyone who might drift in from the highway.

She ate cereal, chopped meat, kidney beans, and noodles. She did just about everything she could to save money, but she was unable to make ends meet. In one city, she came closest to achieving a decent fit between income and expenses, but only because she worked seven days a week. Even there, there was no margin for a new pair of shoes, the loss of the few free meals she got at work, or any unexpected expense. And if you have children, she found, you can't even come close to making it on one salary.

It's not uncommon for poor people to spend more than half their meager monthly incomes on housing, which is the biggest problem. If you can't put up the two months' rent which you need to secure an apartment, you end up paying high for a room by the week. If you have only a room, with a hot plate at best, you can't save by cooking up a huge stew that can be frozen for the week ahead. You eat fast food or the hot dogs and Styrofoam cups of soup that can be microwaved at a convenience store.

These kinds of economic struggles are much more widespread than most people realize. Over the course of a year, nearly a third of poor and working-class families with children under 12 — many with two working parents — face at least one critical hardship, such as being evicted from their home, having their utilities disconnected, doubling up on housing, or not having access to needed medical care.

How to Give

Giving involves not only money, but also time and talent. No matter what we give, it has to be *personal*. Almsgiving is a consciousness-raising session which we can do by ourselves without any professional help. All that governments seem to care about is proclaiming reduced welfare loads. So we can bring food or money saved by fasting to our parish's food pantry or some other food bank. We can volunteer at a local soup kitchen or other shelter. We can get involved with our local political representatives on issues affecting the poor. We can donate not only old clothing, but new items as well.

The desire to give *anonymously* has spiritual roots and a thicket of pragmatic branches. There are many reasons for anonymity. Jesus advised doing good without a flourish of trumpets. Some anonymous donors want to help without burdening the recipient with a sense of indebtedness. Other anonymous donors are allergic to ostentation. The decision to give incognito is often more practical than philosophical: Rich donors don't want to be stampeded by the needy. There's also a Rockefeller effect: the impression that if the megarich are backing a cause, there's no need for checks from others. And there's the "I-am-not-a-Rockefeller" effect: a concern of the donor able to make just one large gift, typically because of a windfall. Others use anonymity as a shield against mischief: They worry that if they found themselves in a lawsuit — after an auto accident, for example — they might be seen as having deep pockets.

Our service and charity to others should at all times be gratuitous, generous, and spontaneous. Freely you have received, freely give. It's significant that the Lord, when he was sending the Apostles to give the first and foremost gift to the human race in spreading the Good News of salvation, reminded them that they had received without paying, so they should give without pay.

Our Poor National Example

Many scholars call the United States the new Rome, meaning an American Empire. Whether this is true or not, we must use our faith tradition to inform and guide our country's position of world superpower. This wealthiest country in the world is also the most stingy. We give last in development aid as a percentage of our Gross Domestic Product. The tiny Caribbean state of Trinidad and Tobago gives nearly 7% of its budget in foreign aid to other needy countries in the Caribbean. We give much less than 1%. The United States gives a mere 75 cents per year per United States citizen toward the United Nations global Fund for AIDS/ Malaria/TB, while every year 8 million people die of these diseases, primarily in poor countries — approximately a Holocaust a year. By comparison, the Pentagon has roughly a $400 billion a year budget.

What do we want the legacy of American Empire to be? All empires end. The Greeks gave us democracy, philosophy, and architecture — all of which we still use and study. The Romans gave us law, aqueducts, roads, architectural arches, republicanism, citizen-soldiers, cuisine, and art that we also use and study today. The British Empire gave us the English language, literature, law, school and public administration, and market economic systems that still serve. What will we leave behind? Plastic bags, dumps of discarded consumer products, happy toys, and patent rights? The Constitution and Declaration of Independence, jazz, rock and roll, the Internet, computers and scientific advancements are certainly contributions. Rockefeller, Ford, and other industrialists bequeathed foundations to pursue a legacy. What do we want to contribute? Much is expected from those to whom much is given (Lk 12:48).

PRAYER

Back in the fifteenth century, in a tiny village near Nuremberg, lived a family with eighteen children. Eighteen! In order merely to keep food on the table, the father, a goldsmith, worked almost eighteen hours a day at his trade and at any other paying job he could find. Despite their seemingly hopeless situation, two of the children of Albrecht Durer the elder had a dream. They both wanted to pursue their talent for art; but they well knew that their father would never be financially able to send either of them to Nuremberg to study at the academy.

After many discussions, the two boys finally worked out a pact. They would toss a coin. The loser would go down into the nearby mines and, with his earnings, support his brother at the academy. Then, when the winner completed his studies in four years, he would support the other brother at the academy, either with the sales of his artwork or, if necessary, also by working in the mines.

They tossed the coin on a Sunday morning after church. Albrecht Durer won the toss and went off to Nuremberg, Albert into the mines. For the next four years, Albert supported his brother, whose work at the academy was an almost immediate sensation. Albrecht's etchings, woodcuts, and oil paintings were far better even than most of his professors'.

When the young artist returned to his village, the Durer family held a festive dinner to celebrate. After a long meal punctuated with music and laughter, Albrecht rose from his honored position at the head of the table to offer a toast to his beloved brother Albert for his years of sacrifice. His closing words were, "And now, Albert, blessed brother of mine, now it's your turn. Now you can go to Nuremberg to pursue your dream, and I will take care of you."

All heads turned in eager expectation to the far end of the table where Albert sat, tears streaming down his pale face, shaking his lowered head from side to side while he sobbed and said, over and over, "No, no, no."

Finally, Albert rose and wiped the tears from his cheeks. He glanced down the long table at the faces he loved, and then said softly, "No, brother. It's too late for me. Look, look what four years in the mines have done to my hands! The bones in every finger have been smashed at least once, and lately I've been suffering from arthritis so bad in my right hand that I can't even hold a glass to return your toast, much less make delicate lines on parchment or canvas with pen or brush. No, brother, for me it's too late!"

One day, to pay homage to Albert for all that he had sacrificed, Albrecht Durer painstakingly drew his brother's abused hands with palms together and thin fingers stretched skyward. Albrecht Durer called his powerful drawing simply "Hands," but the entire world almost immediately opened their hearts to his great masterpiece and renamed his tribute of love, "The Praying Hands." Whereas the joining of hands in prayer didn't appear until around the ninth century, it had become a symbol of man's submission and his lack of inclination to grasp a weapon.

Today, more than 450 years later, Albrecht Durer's hundreds of masterful portraits, sketches, watercolors, charcoals, woodcuts, and copper engravings hang in every great museum in the world. The odds, however, are that most people are familiar with only one of his works — "The Praying Hands." They're a reminder that no one — no one — ever makes it alone. We all need to pray to acknowledge our dependence on God and one another. Lent is a special time to concentrate on prayer.

What to Pray for

What, then, are we to pray for? One model is the nurse who taught a child to pray on his fingers. This was her method. Your thumb is the digit nearest to your heart, so pray first for the family and friends who are closest to you. Your own needs, of course, should be included in that. The second finger is the one used for pointing. Pray for those who point you toward the truth, whether at church or school: your teachers, mentors, pastors, and those who inspire your faith. The third finger is the tallest. Let it stand for the leaders in every sphere of life: those in authority — both within the body of Christ and those who hold office in various areas of government. The fourth finger is the weakest, as every pianist knows. Let it stand for those who are in trouble and pain, sick, injured, abused, wounded, or hurt. The little finger is the smallest. Let it stand for those who often go unnoticed, including those who suffer abuse and deprivation.

Lent is a time when we concentrate our prayer on the double meaning of this season: turning away from our sinful ways and renewal of our baptismal promises by fidelity to the gospel. Private prayer, family prayer, and communal prayer all work together to deepen our spiritual life.

Prayers of Petition

God gets asked for things incessantly. Give me an increase of faith. Give me a job. Give me love. Give me health. Give me a special favor. Give me talent. Give me peace. God gets asked on behalf of others, too. Give my family financial security. Give my spouse gratitude. Give my mother-in-law humility. Give my dying father courage. Give my boss patience. Give my depressed aunt hope. Give my sick friend strength. Give my co-workers serenity. Gimme, gimme, gimme.

In other words, don't just be there, God; do something!

Spiritual writers assure us that God welcomes prayers of petition. God wants to say yes to whatever is truly good for us. Jesus said, "Ask and you shall receive."

But may God not deserve an occasional relief from requests? You and I want to be loved for who we are, not for what we can do. And we're in God's image. So it stands to reason that the Lord may prefer less importuning from us and more adoration. God is love. There are people we love — family and friends and others we're close to — and when we're together, we don't want them always asking us for a favor. If they did that, they'd be less loved ones than nuisances.

Other Forms of Prayer

Besides participating in Mass, there are many forms of prayer. A simple one that is especially appropriate for this season comes from the Eastern tradition of Christianity. It's called the "Jesus prayer." In it, the practitioner breathes in deeply while saying, "Lord Jesus Christ, Son of God," and then breathes out while saying, "have mercy on me, a sinner."

One good practice for Lent might be just to sit for five minutes a day and try to be conscious of God without asking for anything. Perhaps in that time we could thank God for our life, for our loved ones, for the whole human family. In fact, it would be good to make a special effort to think of the things we're thankful for that we may never have thought of before. The mess I have to clean up after a party, because it means I have been surrounded by friends. The taxes I pay, because it means that I'm employed. The clothes that fit a little too snugly, because it means I have enough to eat. The spot I find at the far end of the parking lot, because it means I'm capable of walking. My huge heating bill, because it means I'm warm. The lady behind me in church who sings off key, because it means I'm able to discern. The alarm that goes off in the early morning hours, because it means that I'm alive.

We could tell God of our gratitude for what happened over

the years, both enjoyable and painful, that brought us closer to Him. Maybe we could start the five minutes in God's presence by reading the New Testament to put ourselves in the presence of the Lord. During this five-minute gratitude time, let's not think or pray about what we need or want. Instead, let's tell God that He's already given us a lot, beginning with life itself, and including faith, hope, and love, and that we gratefully accept these wonderful blessings.

WHAT ELSE TO DO FOR LENT

Most people want to serve God, but only in an advisory capacity. Lent is a time for us to reflect on our relationship with the Lord and with people. We remember the invitation given through the prophet Zechariah: "Return to me, says the Lord of Hosts, and I will return to you" (Zc 1:3).

Every one of us needs time for reflection as part of our life. Nobody is exempt. When ashes are placed on our foreheads on Ash Wednesday, we hear the ancient admonition, "Turn away from sin and be faithful to the gospel." We need to reflect and ask, "What should I turn away from? And what do I need to turn my attention to?" How can we turn to our duties in life with more love? That smudge of ashes is leveling: Beneath all our differences, we all need renewal. Possible areas of need are doubts or questions about the faith, personal wounds that have been eating away at us, a spiritual life stuck in neutral. How to proceed, then? Talk about it with people: priest, fellow Christian, family. Read a good book. Share with someone else what we've chosen to do. Encourage one another.

Although complete transformation probably won't occur in one season, a specific area of our life that needs reconstruction can be worked on. Lent is a good time to do something extra. Go to Mass more often. Make visits to the church. Spend more time with your family. Give back something to others. Motivate others to do better. Participate in religious discussions. Give up arguing with your family. Renew your relationship with the Lord. Meet with a prayer group. Give some time to a soup kitchen. Pray for an enemy or someone who has wandered. Take advantage of the frequent opportunities for mortifications in everyday life: in punctuality, in taking care of the things we have, in giving zealous service to even the smallest of our obligations, in smiling (which can often be the best sign of a spirit of penance), and in the moderation with which we indulge in entertainment.

Many people practice penance and self-denial on a large scale for motives other than religious: jogging, attending health clubs, doing aerobic exercises, working with weights, abandoning smoking, giving up hard liquor. And many who rebelled at eating fish on Friday eat more fish on all days to reduce their cholesterol. Much of this shows that Church law and the laws of nature often coincide. Mortification enables us to control our tendency to have a good time as the foremost reason for being alive.

The spirit of mortification that God wants isn't an attitude of rejecting what is good and noble in the things of earth that God has given us to use and enjoy. It's rather a manifestation of supernatural mastery over our body and all created things — human relationships and work, along with everything else. It's not simply privation; rather, it's a manifestation of love. St. Augustine wrote: "To suffer need is something that can happen to anybody, but knowing how to endure it belongs to great souls."

A good part of what to do for Lent is mortifications that make life more pleasant for others — in those things that affect our relationships and dealings. We will try to make people happy even when we have our own problems. St. John Chrysostom said: "many may not find giving up food and drink and a soft bed too difficult.... But bearing an insult, a wrong, or hurtful words ... this is something [that can] be borne not by many but by few."

As well as in these mortifications that refer to charity, God wants us to know how to find Him in all those things He allows to happen which can go against our likes and preferences. These are known as *passive mortifications*. They can take the form of serious illness, or family problems, or major setbacks at work, or little everyday annoyances.

Another field of mortification in which we can show our love for God is in the commendable fulfillment of our duty — by working intensely, for example, and by not leaving unpleasant tasks for later, by struggling against laziness, by taking care of little things like order and punctuality, or by facilitating the tasks of others. Also, the catechetical nature of the season points to paying more attention to Lenten homilies or instructions as particularly appropriate. There are other worthy practices. Daily Mass, the Stations of the Cross, and meditations on the sufferings of Jesus are fitting.

If we want to show special love for God, we might engage in reparation — for the sins of others as well as our own. Reparation is wider and more positive than expiation or satisfaction for sin, in that its burden isn't only the removal of sin and guilt and penalty, but the reestablishment of all things in Christ. It's supererogation — doing more than is required or expected. In the process of reparation, the Christian tries to share in the redemptive mission of Christ, who, by his obedience to the will of his Father in heaven, especially by offering his life on the cross, merited eternal salvation for all the human race. Every offense committed against injustice and truth entails the duty of reparation by someone (*Catechism of the Catholic Church*, #2487). People must restore to God what they have deprived Him of and make amends for the insult done to Him. Some saints, such as Rose of Lima, Thérèse of Lisieux, and Gabriel Possenti, devoted their lives to reparation.

Reparation is contained, actually or virtually, in the mere carrying out of the commandments of God and of the Church.

By reason of one's association in the priesthood of Christ by Baptism, all of the day's actions can be merged with Christ's redemptive action. Also, attendance at Mass with the intention, even obscure, of being united to Christ's sacrifice is a special means for sharing in his work of reparation. Many prayers of reparation, acts of reparation, and the morning offering have been richly indulgenced.

Whatever we decide to do, we have to realize that it has to be individualized. Look at your fingertips. Each one is crowned by an abstract design that's completely different from that of anyone else in the world. That individualization isn't only from one person to another, but even within ourselves from one time to another. We enter each Lent at different stages in our individual journey through life; each Lent is therefore new and different from any other.

Along the path we also encounter joy, because the cross isn't a gallows; it's the throne from which God reigns. As St. Peter of Alcantara said of temperance and mortification, with a pampered and satiated body the soul is not free to fly high.

Turn Away from Sin
and Be Faithful to the Gospel

On a monthly visit to a tropical mission village, a priest was asked to help hearing children's confessions. In lieu of a dark confessional, he opted to sit in a chair under a tree. When the first little penitent approached, he waited for her to begin. She said nothing.

Finally, he asked gently, "Do you want to go to confession?"

"Yes," she replied, but still said nothing.

Growing a bit more firm, he said, "Tell me your sins."

Without hesitating, she asked, "The ones I did or the ones I plan on doing?"

The girl was hardly instructed in the spirit of Lent, which is a time of public and private repentance for our past sins and a resolution to do better in the future. In today's first reading the prophet Joel ordered the whole community to gather the people and notify the congregation for public penance. In the gospel Jesus advises us to make our self-giving, prayer, and fasting a private matter. In today's second reading, St. Paul adds an important note: The time is now. Each of today's readings reminds us that God is ready to take pity on us if we really — "with all our heart" — want to turn away from sins and live by God's message.

The prophecy of Joel was written about 450 years before Christ. A terrible invasion of locusts had ravaged the kingdom of Judah. So frightful was the scourge that the prophet visualized it as a symbol of the coming day of the Lord. In the face of this catastrophe, he summoned the people in God's name to repent for their sins.

Their repentance was to be deeply interior as well as public: The people were to rend their hearts and not just their garments (v. 13). The prophet gives a litany of God's qualities: He's gracious, merciful, slow to anger, rich in kindness, and relenting in punishment. Although (v. 14) God is free and can't be manipulated, His response is not disconnected from the actions of people.

Joel saw *public* repentance as so necessary (v. 15) that he called upon his people to blow the trumpet (*shofar*). Imagine the awe! Trumpets, whether of horn, conch shell, reed, wood, or brass, put forth a majestic sound, originally as a military signal. That exalted sound played a role in many First Testament appearances of God: for instance, at the assembly of God's people at Sinai, and the sound of trumpets bringing down the walls of Jericho. God's trumpet will accompany the scene of Christ's second coming.

In the gospel, which is from Jesus' Sermon on the Mount outlining some of the essence of Christianity, he teaches his followers how to practice prayer, fasting, and almsgiving: not to be praised by others but to be seen and acknowledged by our heavenly Father. Yet Jesus, in calling for people to keep their deeds of mercy secret, doesn't contradict Joel's call for a public period of fasting and mourning. Both Joel and Jesus summon all of us to act as a family of love.

What, then, to do for Lent? In addition to "giving up" things, it would be good to be positive. One way is to prepare for reconciliation — with God, with one another, and with ourselves. On an immediate level, the need for reconciliation can show itself in family rows, neighbors not communicating because of some incident long forgotten, words that have caused hurt, or disgust over how we see ourselves. There can be no peace without reconciliation.

Triumph can be accomplished especially in the *sacrament* of Reconciliation. The concept of the self has developed over the centuries. Without a sense of the self, there could be no confession, and without the requirement of confession there would be no exploration of this selfhood. Confession presupposes inner depths and hidden secrets, no matter who is trying to get at them — inquisitor, confessor, psychiatrist, talk-show host, or cop.

Without intending to, the Church created the earliest model of the modern self with its *id* and unconscious (the secrets created by passion and hidden in shame), the *ego* of the self who is free to choose between self-revelation or concealment, and the *superego*, whether forgiving father confessor or the bars of justice. Facing oneself is something that we must do individually. Look at your fingertips. Each one is crowned by a design that's completely different from that of anyone else in this world. Each of us is as different from everyone else as our fingertips.

Pope Paul VI defined a sacrament as "a reality imbued with the hidden presence of God." God's presence in the sacrament of Penance, or Reconciliation, or Confession — whatever we're in the habit of calling it — is quite apparent. Every time we go to this sacrament we acknowledge that we have culpable sins; we affirm that through the mercy of God sin is forgivable; we implicitly testify that God's merciful forgiveness comes through the priest from Jesus; we attest that the Church is a mother who loves us, even when we can't love ourselves; we implicitly confirm that God wants us to reject a part of our past life; we experience God reaching out to welcome sinners home to renewed relationships with Him, with community, and with ourselves; and we implicitly reaffirm that we can do things with God's grace that we mightn't succeed in doing on our own.

Lent isn't a business-as-usual season: It's a significant part of our life as Christians. If we don't accept St. Paul's admonition not to receive the grace of God in vain, we're missing a golden opportunity to deepen our commitment to Jesus. Because Lent is a Springtime that gives us opportunities for spiritual flowering and growth, it's a joyful season. Our Lenten journey, which we begin today, doesn't end in sadness on Good Friday, but in the joyful integration of Easter.

Making the Right Choices

A man who studied gravestone markings in cemeteries around New England made an odd, but revealing, finding. In the seventeenth, eighteenth, and nineteenth centuries, the vast preponderance of the grave markings related to character: that the interred had been a loving father, a devoted mother, a brave man, a courageous woman. In the twentieth century the vast preponderance of the inscriptions mention not character but profession. Yet character is what defines us — and character is made by our choices.

Our choice in today's first reading is easy. Moses sets before us a choice between life and death. We choose life, of course, instead of death; a blessing rather than a curse; a happy life rather than a miserable one. But for us to say we choose life means that we set in motion a parcel of other choices: to obey God's commandments, to walk in the ways of the Lord, to hold fast to the Lord.

In the crowds whom Jesus had won over by his words and his kindness, were there many who were ready to follow him under any conditions? To them, he said that whether anyone wants to come after him is voluntary. The most astonishing thing about God's creative activity is that He makes us free — free even to accept or reject the Creator Himself.

But once people accept God, they must know that He then expects an ascent of one's soul into higher realms. That ascent begins with denying one's very self. Because now our life has a new meaning and a higher purpose, we must say "no" to self and "yes" to God. The highest point of our ascent arrives when we take up our crosses, whatever they may be, out of the joy that follows upon love. At the time Jesus spoke these words, the cross was the symbol of the ultimate degradation, a wretched punishment meted out to the most monstrous criminals. The Torah, in fact, had said that God's *curse* rested upon anyone who was crucified (Dt 21:23). So Jesus was going against all received opinions, and wasn't offering an easy way; but he wasn't asking anyone to do what he wouldn't first do himself.

Then Jesus said what a careful advertiser, trying to set out his ideas in an attractive order, might have put first: All those who wish to save their life will lose it, but all who lose their life for his sake and that of the gospel will save it. History is full of examples of people — especially generous youth — who, by spending their life for others, saved it, and whose death was more useful to the human race than their life. People who think first of their own profit, comfort, or security are losing life every moment of their search, whereas those who forget themselves to spend their lives for Jesus and for those for whom he died are winning life all the time. To lose one's life for the sake of Jesus is in fact to save it just as his sacrifice of life was followed by resurrection.

Such are pioneers who explore new horizons, women who accept the risk of bearing children, missionaries who don't remain comfortably at home, scientists who spend their lives for others. They find that the way to happiness and fulfillment is to live life to the full rather than have it just fritter away. In the final analysis, the solution to the question of the encounter between suffering and joy is to love greatly, because if we truly love we find joy in sacrificing for the beloved.

Jesus' words have rung through the ages as not simply good Christianity, but — as we come to know more about human beings through some of our newer sciences — good psychology as well: Whoever wishes to save his life will lose it, but whoever loses his life for Jesus' sake will find it (v. 25). Most of the arts, sciences, and professions center around human beings. Physicians study the body; lawyers try to secure justice; psychiatrists try to interpret people's innermost drives; sociologists derive understanding from group conduct; historians arrive at conclusions from humankind's record. But not too many people put it all together to come up with overall suggestions for the best way to live. Today's gospel is one example among many of Jesus putting together the wisdom of the ages.

There's a difference between *existing* and *living*. The path to worldliness, and to spiritual destruction — which means just existing — begins with small steps: I'm too busy, too tired, not ready. Someone once bitterly wrote on the tombstone of another, "He was born a man and died a merchant." If we substitute for "merchant" our own position — manager, clerk, lawyer, housewife, student, laborer — we might ask ourselves whether we've spent so much time on unimportant things that we've become less a person: in other words whether somewhere along the line we've lost our "self." The mentally healthiest are those who have never stopped finding ways to lose themselves in other people for Jesus' sake. At the same time, we must balance this out with other parts of the Scriptures, where Jesus advises us to exercise our responsibilities: to pay off our debts, for example, and to take care of our family and help improve world conditions.

It's a question of balance, as Jesus illustrates in his asking what profit would there be for us to gain the whole world and forfeit our self, or what can we give in exchange for our self. The selling or giving away of self happens every day — with "yes-men" who curry favor with their bosses, with the weak who surrender themselves to stronger personalities, with those who have never developed any lasting principles to guide their lives. Once we've sold ourselves or given ourselves away, our most precious possession — our "self" — is gone, and it becomes extremely difficult to get it back.

The profession of faith and the practice of good works are, like joy and sorrow, not an "either-or" proposition; they're a "both-and" proposition. The well-designed life has both joy and sorrow, thought and action. A life of joy with no sorrow can become like a terrain with all sunshine and no rain: a barren desert. Both suffering and joy, and both faith and good works, are necessary for the life of the good Christian.

Friday after Ash Wednesday
Is 58:1-9; Mt 9:14f.

True and False "Fasting"

There's a story, now famous within social justice circles, about a town that was built just beyond the bend of a large river. One day some of the children from the town were playing beside the river when they noticed three bodies floating in the water. They ran for help and the townspeople quickly pulled the bodies out of the river. One body was dead, so they buried it. One was alive, but quite ill, so they put that person in the hospital. The third turned out to be a healthy child, whom they placed with a caring family.

From that day on, every day a number of bodies came floating down the river and, every day, the good people of the town pulled them out and tended to them — taking the sick to hospitals, placing the children with families, and burying those who were dead.

That went on for years. The townspeople not only came to expect a number of bodies each day, but also worked to develop more elaborate systems for picking them out of the river and tending to them. The town came to feel a healthy pride in its generosity.

During all these years, however, and despite all that generosity and effort, nobody thought to go up the river, beyond the bend that hid from their sight what was above them, and find out why, daily, those bodies came floating down the river.

The story highlights the difference between mere "fasting" and the positive practices that the Lord wants. Fasting has an important place in all the great religions. The Jewish Scriptures list fasting among the cornerstones of the spirituality of Israel. "Prayer is good when accompanied by fasting, almsgiving, and justice" (Tb 12:8). Fasting, inseparable from prayer and justice, is directed above all to conversion of heart, without which it's meaningless. Before beginning his public mission, Jesus was driven by the Holy Spirit to fast for forty days as an expression of his trusting abandonment to the heavenly Father's saving plan (cf. Mt 4:1-4). He gave precise instructions to his disciples that their fasting should never be tainted by ostentation and hypocrisy (cf. Mt 6:16-18).

Fasting is closely connected to prayer; it strengthens virtue, inspires mercy, implores divine assistance and leads to conversion of heart. It's in this double sense — imploring the grace of the Almighty and profound inner conversion — that we're called to fast.

The practice of fasting looks to the past, present, and future: to the past, as a recognition of offenses committed against God and others; to the present, in order that we may learn to open our eyes to others and to the world around us; to the future, in order that we may open our hearts to the realities of God and, by the gift of divine mercy, renew the bond of communion with all people and with the whole of creation, accepting our personal responsibility.

Our Lenten fast has less to do with dieting than with Isaiah's description of it as works of social justice, such as freeing the oppressed, sheltering the homeless, clothing the naked, and sharing our bread with the hungry. Fasting isn't just eating less, but doing more. Of the "pious" who do no more than just praying about the world's ills, someone has written a parody: I was hungry, and you formed a humanities group to discuss my hunger. I was imprisoned, and you crept off to your chapel and prayed for my release. I was naked, and in your mind you debated the morality of my appearance. I was sick, and you knelt and thanked God for your health. I was homeless, and you preached to me of the spiritual shelter of the love of God. I was lonely, and you left me alone to pray for me. You seem so holy, so close to God. But I am still very hungry — and lonely — and cold.

True "fasting" responds to the dead bodies, but also tries to get at the reasons why the problems are there. Christian social justice demands that we look around the bend in the river and change the conditions that create the dead bodies. That's what Lent has in mind. The statistics on the needy of our country and the world are mind-boggling — we in the United States have so much more than others!

Fasting is an act of self-denial. People fast partly in order to overcome an indulgent spirit which seeks comfort and pleasure above all else. With this in mind, we can begin to understand why the prophet Isaiah railed against his people. Their prescribed fast day had become a farce, for while they purported to be denying themselves, inwardly they were as self-seeking and ruthless as ever. The real fast — the one which truly honors God — is the self-denial expressed in deeds of justice and compassion, in freeing the oppressed, in sharing one's bread with the hungry.

Whereas our excerpt from Isaiah centers on fasting, the prophet's purpose is much broader. Merely external worship, says Isaiah (vv. 2-14), doesn't avail with God; it must spring from internal sincerity. Even though the people say they seek the Lord, ironically their disposition turns them away from precisely that search (vv. 2-4). True fasting enables comfortable people to share the lot of the hungry poor and from this hunger to look to God as the source of life and nourishment (v. 5). To fast and yet neglect the poor perverts religion. When lowliness unites all men and women, God's glorious presence shall rest upon them.

The outcome of the final judgment mentioned by Jesus elsewhere (Mt 25:31-46) depends on the kindly acts mentioned by Isaiah here (v. 7). In today's gospel Jesus tells his questioners that whereas the initial experience of his message with its power to heal and liberate was not a time for fasting, there will be times when fasting is appropriate. That time is now.

Consonant with Isaiah and Jesus, an anonymous writer suggests how to fast and feast:

> Fast from judging others; feast on Christ dwelling
>   in them.
> Fast from emphasis on differences; feast on the unity
>   of all life.
> Fast from words that pollute; feast on phrases that purify.
> Fast from discontent; feast on gratitude.
> Fast from anger; feast on patience.
> Fast from pessimism; feast on optimism.
> Fast from complaining; feast on appreciation.
> Fast from negatives; feast on affirmatives.
> Fast from hostility; feast on non-resistance.
> Fast from bitterness; feast on forgiveness.
> Fast from self-concern; feast on compassion for others.
> Fast from discouragement; feast on hope.
> Fast from lethargy; feast on enthusiasm.
> Fast from suspicion; feast on truth.
> Fast from thoughts that weaken; feast on promises
>   that inspire.
> Fast from idle gossip; feast on purposeful silence.
> Fast from problems that overwhelm; feast on prayer
>   that sustains.

Is 58:9-14; Lk 5:27-32

Not for the Self-Righteous,
but Sinners

When Hendrickje Stoffels, Rembrandt's housekeeper, became pregnant with his daughter Cornelia, the artist suffered one of his severest public humiliations. The pregnancy exposed their illicit relationship and outraged the Dutch Reformed community in Amsterdam, to which Rembrandt and Hendrickje belonged. The two were summoned before the church council, repri-manded, and banned from sharing the Lord's Supper — a ban that, as far as parish records go, was never lifted.

It was during the Christmas season of that same year, 1654, that Rembrandt etched his Christmas *Adoration of the Shepherds*. This isn't just a pious picture: Rembrandt was giving an answer. Now he began to see Jesus as a human being, the Son of Human-ity, the humble servant, deeply disgraced. Rembrandt asserted that the mystery of the Incarnation lies precisely in the revela-tion of God's love in the most ordinary of human signs: a desti-tute child lying on straw in a barn, sleeping in a corner reserved for cattle, next to his shabbily clothed mother. Everything in the picture bespeaks stark poverty. Yet the child on the straw shines as the source of light, and of everyone's faith.

It's not a coincidence that Rembrandt chose this scene to make his statement. Reading Luke's gospel, he had been struck by the fact that those invited to see the new Messiah were com-mon shepherds. On whose side did God stand? Did God favor the respectable and prosperous merchants who controlled the boards of church elders?

In Rembrandt's etching, perhaps the three shepherds lean-ing on the wooden partition just next to the child portray Rembrandt himself, his pregnant partner Hendrickje, and his 13-

year-old son Titus. They've been banned from church, but here they're made to feel at home. St. Joseph, seated on a wheelbarrow, shows what the local preacher should be. Instead of issuing a reprimand, he opens his hands in a gesture of genuine welcome. Perhaps Joseph is also saying, "See, the child is what matters. Believe in God Who is Love, and all shall be well." It may well be that Rembrandt was coming more and more to see his own religious search as a personal response to a God who loves even social outcasts.

If in the etching Rembrandt is the man in the middle bending over the child with a look of faith, we note that he's taking off his cap, the typical gesture of a man acknowledging respect, the poor man's attempt at adoration. Perhaps, in this *Adoration of the Shepherds*, Rembrandt offers a plea to the newborn Jesus, praying for acceptance in spite of his being a sinner and having been officially branded as such.

Rembrandt drew comfort from the fact that Jesus, as he says in today's gospel, had come to give hope not to the righteous, but to sinners like himself (v. 32). Today's gospel affords a good contrast between the proud and the unaccepted. It's a story about a tax collector named Levi (or Matthew), who was sitting at a customs post (v. 27). In the Roman system, there were all kinds of taxes: income tax, poll tax, tax on produce, import tax, export tax, road use tax, sales tax, wheel tax on carts, pack animal tax, and more. Tax collectors bid for their positions: They promised to pay a certain amount to Rome and were allowed to line their pockets with the remainder. Not satisfied with this, many tax collectors took bribes from the rich in return for decreasing their taxes, and made up for it against the poor.

The people's hatred of tax collectors was more than a matter of finance. The Jews believed that their God, not Rome or any other power, was their only legitimate king. They barred tax collectors from the synagogue, declared them unclean, and forbade them to act as witnesses in court. Levi loved money enough to have defied all that. His tax-collecting post, a good one, was at Capernaum, on the border where the Jordan River entered the Lake of Galilee and the great road from Egypt to Damascus passed through. His "take" was large.

Jesus saw Levi, not merely in the usual sense, but more significantly with his merciful understanding of people: Jesus' invitation to follow him meant imitating the pattern of his life — not just walking after him. When Levi heard Jesus' call he weighed everything in the balance — his material losses over and against his potential spiritual gains — and he decisively opted for Jesus. Perhaps that was part of the good that Jesus saw in him. He saw in Levi not only who he then was, but who he could become. Fortunately, Jesus does this with all of us.

The immediacy of Levi's response to Jesus' call (v. 28), psychologically implausible, presupposes some prior knowledge of Jesus and his mission and some reflection on his possible place in that mission. The gospel's conciseness is explainable by the demands of oral transmission and the cumbersome method of book production at the time the gospel was written.

Present at Levi's celebratory party (v. 29) were members of despised trades thought susceptible of ritual uncleanness and other blemishes. One list of such people names ass-driver, camel-driver, sailor, caster for fish, herdsman, shopkeeper, physician (because of being a blood letter?), butcher, tanner, bath-attendant, and tax collector. Like Rembrandt in his time, these people in Jesus' time were looked upon as sinners.

Levi's people — Damon Runyon characters all — were perhaps his lifelong friends. Jesus' sharing a meal with sinners seems to have been a genuine practice of his. Here he clearly broke with the model of the Pharisaic sage, in order to save its increasingly marginalized members.

The Pharisees were aghast at a good Jew eating with foreigners, much less with sinners. They didn't enter the dining room. Nor did they have the courage to confront Jesus himself;

they took his *disciples* aside and questioned *them* about why Jesus acted as he did. Jesus, reacting strongly to their snobbishness, tersely leveled them. First, Jesus said, the Pharisees prescribed from afar for fear of contagion, but he, like a good physician, went where sickness caused the greatest need. His mission was not to those who were self-righteous, but to sinners who recognized themselves to be in need of salvation.

The results of Levi/Matthew accepting Jesus' invitation were tremendous. For one thing, without Matthew and his gospel we would be missing such memorable biblical stories as the visit of the wise men, the star of Bethlehem, the flight into Egypt, and the massacre of the holy innocents. Without his gospel we would not have many portions of the Sermon on the Mount. Without him and his gospel we would not have that special name of Jesus: Emmanuel, which means "God is with us." Levi/Matthew the tax-collector knew again that God is with us when he heard Jesus say, "I have come to call, not the self-righteous, but sinners." Levi/Matthew knew that God would be with us not just for a little time, but forever — so he concluded his gospel with Jesus saying, "And know that I am with you always, until the end of the world."

If we can substitute our acquisitive nature, our greed, and our thirst for authority over others, and devote our time to helping those who have less, as today's reading from Isaiah advises and our gospel demonstrates, our world would truly become the Promised Land. Jesus addresses his invitation to Levi to follow him to each of us. What are we waiting for?

The first thing we must do is admit our sinfulness — no excuses, no claims, no self-complacency. And we must confess our inability to get out of our situation of sinfulness by ourselves and admit our absolute need for God's saving power in Jesus. We must constantly beware of self-righteousness because it leads to the kind of blindness and hardness of heart that afflicted the Pharisees.

God's Criteria for Judging Us

There's a story of a woman who had been used to every luxury and to all respect. She died, and when she arrived in heaven an angel was sent to conduct her to her house there. They passed many a lovely mansion, and the woman thought that each one as they came to it must be the one allotted to her. They passed through the main streets, came to the outskirts where the houses were much smaller, and on the very fringe came to a house which was little more than a shack.

"This is your house," said the conducting angel.

"What?" said the woman. "I can't live in that!"

"I'm sorry," said the angel, "but that's all we could build for you with the materials you sent up."

Both of today's Scripture readings concern God's criteria for judging us. But there are differences in each reading's approach. Leviticus is decidedly negative. Notice all the "nots": "You shall *not* steal," and so on. The gospel is positive: "You gave me food — drink — welcomed me — clothed me — and so on." To enter Jesus' kingdom, we need to do much more than eliminate the negative: We have to accentuate the positive.

Another difference between the two readings is in the way the Lord is involved in human conduct. In Leviticus, the motivation for the prescribed deeds is in the refrain, "I am the Lord." In the gospel, the motivation is in the refrain, "You did it for me." We take the quantum leap from the up-there-and-out-there God who declares "I am the Lord" to the immediate, imminent, up-close Son of God who says "You did it for me" — because I am in those whom you feed, welcome, and clothe.

The "Holiness Code" of Leviticus offers as a constant reason for the laws it imposes the imitation of God's unique holiness: "Be holy, for I, the Lord, your God, am holy." God is holy — totally set apart from and above everything else — and He expects His people to be holy, too. Holiness — which is not just otherworldliness — precludes any spirit of enmity, revenge, and grudge-bearing, all of which often seem to be a basic human instinct. A little child's answer about the meaning of holiness was: "Being holy means that you do what your mother says the first time she asks."

Leviticus' Holiness Code contains the most famous line in the book: "Love your neighbor as yourself" (v. 18). Jesus used this law, together with a Jewish prayer (Dt 6:5), to sum up the whole of the Law and the Prophets. It was Jesus who gave the word "neighbor" its universal meaning. In his concept, our neighbor is everyone created by God — everyone for whom he would die. Neither alien nor foe can be excluded. Jesus doesn't ask that we love our enemies as we love our closest friends. Our love for our enemies — those we don't like or who don't like us — isn't of the heart but of the will. To love them needn't be an *emotional* experience, but must be a decision to commit ourselves to serve the best interests of all other people.

The gospel reminds us that Jesus came to preach good news to the poor. "Jesus shares the life of the poor, from the cradle to the cross; he experiences hunger, thirst, privation. Jesus identifies himself with the poor of every kind and makes active love of them the condition for entering his kingdom." (*Catechism of the Catholic Church*, #544.)

Jesus tells us that the sole criterion for his eventual judgment of us is our exercise of love. Love is the meaning of life. It's the essence of what God showed us in Christ. It's our opportunity for fulfillment. What's done out of love lasts forever — the *only* thing that lasts forever. The chances to express it are all around us.

Jesus illustrates his criterion with simple things that are not unlike the story of the "Keeper of the Spring," who lived high above an Austrian village in the Alps. The old gentleman was hired to clear away the debris from the pools of water up in the mountain spring that fed the lovely stream flowing through their village. With faithful regularity he removed the leaves and branches and wiped away the silt that would otherwise have contaminated the fresh flow of water. The village soon became a popular attraction for vacationers. Graceful swans floated along the crystal clear stream, the mill wheels of various businesses located near the water turned day and night, farmlands were irrigated naturally, and the view from restaurants was picturesque beyond description.

Years passed. One evening, the town council met. As they reviewed the budget, a member's eye caught the salary figure being paid the obscure keeper of the spring. He asked, "Who's this old man? No one ever sees him. For all we know, he's doing no good. Why do we keep him on year after year?" By unanimous vote, they dispensed with the old man's services.

Nothing changed right away. By early autumn, the trees began to shed their leaves. Small branches snapped off and fell into the pools, hindering the rushing flow of sparkling water. One afternoon someone noticed a slight yellowish-brown tint in the spring. A few days later, the water was much darker. Within another week, a slimy film covered sections of the water along the banks, and a foul odor was detected. The mill wheels moved more slowly, some grinding to a halt. Swans left, as did the tourists.

Quickly, the embarrassed council called a special meeting. Realizing their gross error in judgment, they rehired the old keeper of the spring, and within a few weeks the river began to clear up. The wheels started to turn, and new life returned to their hamlet.

The story reminds us to cling to the words of Edward Everett Hale: "I am only one, but still I am one. I cannot do everything, but still I can do something; and because I cannot do everything, I will not refuse to do something I can do." The key to accomplishment is believing that what we can do will make a difference. The simple things that Jesus asks, everybody can do: feeding the hungry, giving thirsty people a drink, making strangers welcome, providing covering for the ill-clothed, comforting the sick, and visiting those in jail.

All of these can be interpreted literally: The whole world has more than its share of the homeless, the hungry, and the otherwise needy. But often we're called to meet needs which require looking below the surface and demand creativity and initiative. With the hungry, creativity and initiative may suggest feeding people's hunger for knowledge by volunteering at a literacy organization, feeding people's hunger for companionship by welcoming a new neighbor in for coffee, or feeding the hunger for intimacy by lending our ear to people in need of sympathy. Looking below the surface may suggest slaking people's thirst for justice by contacting legislators about issues of concern, or people's thirst for equality by not discriminating, or people's thirst for self-worth by helping battered spouses or other people on the edge.

We can welcome the stranger by helping at a shelter for the troubled, by teaching children to accept people of all colors and cultures, or by volunteering at a hotline for people with problems. To clothe the naked, we might supply a poor family with such essentials for good grooming as soap, detergent, toothpaste, or cosmetics. We might visit the sick by helping people who suffer from substance abuse, or listening to a friend who is depressed. As for prison, we can help people who are locked up by the conditions of their lives: materialism, loneliness, loss of a sense of their human dignity and of hope about the meaning of their lives.

Actually, the list of the "corporal works of mercy" are limitless. If we have compassionate hearts we will see many ways to be of help to people who need us. To emphasize the actions' importance, Jesus goes through the scene a second time, from the viewpoint of the condemned. His listeners' surprise (v. 44) is easy to understand: They never accepted the idea of encountering Jesus in other people. Too often people's attitude is: "If only I'd known it was *you*, I'd have helped."

Jesus is in the unattractive. No matter how repulsive some people may appear to us, Jesus identifies himself with *all* who need to be served. And he doesn't say that he will *consider* these things as done to him; he says it *is* done to him (v. 40). Mother Teresa said, "If sometimes our poor people have had to die out of starvation, it is not because God didn't care for them, but because you and I... were not instruments of love in the hands of God, because we did not recognize Christ, when once more Christ came in distressing disguise." And we find that kindness is difficult to give away because it keeps coming back.

At the beginning of Lent we again get a reminder that good works are, with prayer and fasting, essential to our proper observance of the season. For the Christian, the achievement of Christ's kingdom in the world begins not when we give others what they have a right to, which is justice; it begins when we go beyond justice to accept others as persons by seeing Christ in them, and then giving them ourselves, which is love. The sound of the silence that accompanies inaction is deafening.

Beginning now, let's treat all whom we meet as if they — or we — were going to be dead by midnight. Extend to them all the care, kindness, and understanding we can muster, and do so with no thought of any reward. Our life will never be the same.

Is 55:10f.; Mt 6:7-15

Prayer and How to Do It

Isaiah, whose poems teem with courageous hopes and persistent ideals, here symbolizes the cycle of life by rain and snow falling gently from the sky and soaking the earth with nourishment, then returning toward heaven when it has nourished seed for flowers, bushes, and trees, producing abundant growth. The water also returns to the sea by way of streams and rivers. The cycle resumes as the water in the sea again evaporates back into the clouds. The clouds don't simply hang motionless in the sky, but let their rain fall upon the thirsty earth. *Our* rain and snow is the word of God, our bushes and trees our graced lives.

In order that our tender growth reach toward God over time, God's interior life within us must be delicately nourished by love — the type of love which Jesus teaches us in the *Lord's Prayer*. His beautiful words — of nearby heaven, of kingdom come, of sweet-smelling fresh bread, of gentle forgiveness from depths of understanding, of deliverance from all anxiety, of soothing every wrong — inspire a delicate new life with warmth, hope, and love, and make us fully-formed people of God.

Jesus' disciples had seen how his prayer illumined his countenance. And they were aware that religious groups were marked by their own prayer forms. The disciples wanted their own "Identification Prayer" too: a distinctive badge that would bind them together and be an expression of their chief beliefs. So they timidly asked Jesus to teach them to pray in the same way as he did, hoping for the same radiance they saw in him when he prayed.

Jesus answered by giving them this prayer which, in its simplicity, contrasts sharply with many of the very fulsome formulations used in Jewish and Greco-Roman prayers of his day, not to mention some of today's equivalents. Tertullian called the

Lord's Prayer, despite its brevity, "truly a summary of the whole Gospel." In it we ask, not only for all the things we can rightly desire, but also in the sequence that they should be desired (*Catechism of the Catholic Church*, #2763, citing St. Thomas Aquinas).

Reverent approach to God, once the domain of priests and Levites, now became open to all. And we can approach confidently, because Jesus has sympathy for us and taught us that we have a loving God in heaven. We often forget that the biblical expression of our Father "who art in heaven" doesn't mean a place, but a way of being: It doesn't mean that God is distant, but majestic (*Catechism of the Catholic Church,* #2794). We often forget, too, that the ideas about God given us by Jesus are completely new. For the Jews, God was holy — and therefore separate, apart, different. The gods of the Greeks were even more aloof. We're lucky to have had Jesus teach us about the true God and how we can best live our lives in imitating and serving Him.

The Lord's Prayer has all the major elements of prayer: adoration, contrition, thanksgiving, and supplication ("ACTS"). Because a vital part of our prayer — not the only part — is supplication, that's what the Lord's Prayer demonstrates most.

A simplistic example of prayer of supplication is the little girl, dressed in her Sunday best, running as fast as she could, trying not to be late for Bible class. As she ran she prayed, "Dear Lord, please don't let me be late! Dear Lord, please don't let me be late!" As she was running and praying, she tripped on a curb and fell, getting her clothes dirty and tearing her dress. She got up, brushed herself off, and started running again. As she ran, she once again began to pray, "Dear Lord, please don't let me be late!... But please don't shove me, either!"

That's an illustration that God doesn't always answer our prayers in the way we would initially like them to be. As the anonymous scholar put it, "Some people complain that God put thorns on roses, while others praise Him for putting roses on thorns."

Instead of moving prayers too often in a circle around our own small "I," our own needs and troubles and desires, Jesus teaches us to ask also for the *great* things — for God's almighty glory and kingdom, and that God's great gifts and His endless mercy may be granted us. The very first word — *Father* — transports us at once into a new era: God our Father, life of the faithful, glory of the humble, happiness of the just.

Studies have found that our concept of God is based on our experience with our earthly father. We mightn't hold out much hope for the little boy who with a companion was walking home from Sunday school after hearing a strong sermon on the devil. His friend said to him, "What do you think about all this Satan stuff?" The other boy replied, "Well, you know how Santa Claus turned out. It's probably just your dad."

Other people find difficulty with the word *Father* as the name for God as being too male-chauvinist. But the Fatherhood of God in the Jewish Scriptures contains also something of what the word "Mother" signifies to us: tenderness, mercy, care, and love. In the gospels we find the word "Father" for God on the lips of Jesus 170 times.

Though we may take the privilege of calling God *Father* for granted, the early Christians were thrilled that they were allowed to use the word. He with whom Jesus wants us to speak in prayer is less the creator of the universe, the Lord of heaven and earth, than *Abba*, "dad," a diminutive term of endearment that was used by adults as well as children for their own fathers: *the* word that could express most adequately the most intimate, most personal relationship anyone could think of.

Jesus didn't intend what he gave to be our *only* prayer, but the *model* of prayer. Like choosing our clothing for the day, prayer is one of the things we all have to do on our own. No one else can do it for us. Speaking with God is an intensely personal event. Lent is a good time to improve it.

There are many helpful hints for doing personal prayer well.

First, it's good to set the same time each day — a time when we're most at ease — to uninterruptedly communicate with the Lord. Secondly, our prayer should be from our heart — not just a re- citing of ideas, even though perhaps written by great saints, in which we think God would like to hear. Thirdly, we should await the Lord's response. After a while, we'll be tuned into the Holy Spirit and won't be greeted by silence.

Always, it's in a spirit of silence that prayer is best. Mother Teresa said that silence will teach us to speak with Christ and to speak joyfully to our brothers and sisters. She also said that God is the friend of silence, and pointed out that nature — trees, flowers, grass — grow in silence. And Thomas Merton published the fact that it was in deep silence that he found the gentleness with which he could truly love people as his brothers and sisters.

Many people who faithfully pray expect an answer like the *deus ex machina* on the stage of the ancient Greeks. That was a piece of stage apparatus that the dramatists sometimes used to pluck a character in distress, for whom the playwright could find no other resolution, from the stage by a friendly god — an un- believable resolution to a problem.

Like listening, preaching, or teaching, we have to start at some point with prayer, then slowly improve.

Wednesday, First Week of Lent

Jon 3:1-10; Lk 11:29-32

Hope

Some people are hard to convince. At times, that includes our- selves. The scribes and Pharisees refused to accept the miracles of Jesus as authentication of his claims and demanded that he

show a sign that his authority was approved. Because Jesus knew
that nothing would convince his evil opponents, his response was
that no such sign would be given except Jonah in the fish — the
sign of his resurrection. It's a fitting sign for Lent: It reminds us
of hope, both in the conversion of the Ninevites in the Book of
Jonah and in Jesus' resurrection at Easter.

Jonah's life goes back to the eighth century B.C., but his
story was written four or five hundred years later. Is his story
true in the sense of having actually happened? Not every aspect.
Does the story present truth? Yes! In the Scriptures, we find every kind of literature — poetry, prose, history, allegory, fable —
and short stories, of which Jonah is one. It's the nature of such
folk-tales (like Cinderella or Snow White) to present some truth.

Jonah didn't want God to show mercy to the Gentile
Assyrian Ninevite foreigners to whom God had sent him. In the
mind of good (but narrow) Jews of that time, these were the worst
possible barbarians — so let them be destroyed! Jonah very much
wanted his eight-word warning to come true: "Forty days more
and Nineveh shall be destroyed."

Jonah tried to escape God's assignment to preach to the
Ninevites by boarding a ship. The ship was tossed about by a
storm. When Jonah confessed to the superstitious sailors that he
was their jinx, they threw him overboard. The story has it that
he was swallowed by a huge fish; when after three days he was
freed, he decided that, considering what he'd gone through, going to Nineveh wouldn't be all that bad after all! So he went.

The paining Jonah wasn't unhappy to announce that
Nineveh would be destroyed unless its people repented (v. 4).
Much to Jonah's chagrin and amazement, the Ninevites, from the
king to the lowest peasant, did repent (v. 5), and prayed for mercy
— as Jerusalem never did — and God didn't carry out His threats
(v. 10). It's a spectacular story of conversion, repentance, and
salvation. Luckily for sinners, it's not up to Jonah, or us, to decide who is or isn't worthy of salvation.

The Book of Jonah provides the most wonderful of surprises: the extraordinary and unsuspected goodness of even such unlikely candidates for holiness as the ever-hated Assyrians (or our worst enemy, or the most impossible sinner we can imagine). We must never lose hope in the tremendous depths of hidden goodness in others and in ourselves. So it was at the preaching of Jonah, and we have a greater than Jonah in Jesus.

Lent is the season that calls us to turn our hearts to God. "Jesus' call to conversion and penance, like that of the prophets before him, does not aim first at outward works, sackcloth and ashes, fasting and mortification, but at the conversion of heart, interior conversion" (*Catechism of the Catholic Church*, #430). This interior conversion is a radical turning away from sin and evil in our lives.

It may, however, be necessary for some of us to remember that sin isn't the end of the world — and, in fact, may actually be the beginning of a number of things that can be gained hardly any other way. A bout with greed may be precisely what teaches us the freedom of poverty. A struggle with lust may well be what teaches us about the real nature of love. From owning up to our sins we might learn some qualities that are hard to come by, like compassion, understanding, humility, and sensitivity. The critical point is: Are we, like the ancient Ninevites, able to change?

We must have hope. Some people in Kenya say that a dog in the water that sees the shore doesn't drown. We have to show the shore to everyone in difficulty. Hope is a cornerstone of our religion. We can say, along with St. Paul in his Letter to the Romans (8:25), that we hope for what we don't see and we wait for it with patience. The Letter to the Hebrews (6:19) tells us that hope is the steadfast anchor of the soul. The prophets remind us that all who dream of justice and peace and healing must be steeped in hope. St. Augustine said, "Hope has two daughters — anger and courage. Anger at the way things are, and courage to work to make things other than they are." That can lead to transformation.

Transformation is a marvelous thing. Think especially of a butterfly. There comes for every caterpillar a difficult moment when he begins to feel pervaded by an odd sense of discomfort. Even though he has molted a few times before, that is nothing in comparison to the urge that he feels now. He must shed his tight dry skin or die.

The caterpillar walks about looking for a suitable place to hang from in the open air. He crawls up a wall or a tree trunk. He hangs himself by the tip of his tail or back legs, so as to dangle head downward. His question now is how to get rid of his skin. One wriggle, another wriggle — and zip, the skin bursts down the back. He gradually gets out if it working with shoulders and hips like a person getting out of a sausage garment.

Very carefully this courageous and stubborn little animal starts dislodging his hind legs from the patch of silk from which he is dangling head down. Then, with a twist and a jerk, he sheds his last shred of skin, and immediately in the process attaches himself anew to the tree by means of a hook that was under the tip of his body. Now the bared surface, hard and glistening, becomes the pupa — a beautiful chrysalis.

The pupa hangs quite motionless, but one day after, say, two or three weeks, through his tiny wing cases you can see in miniature the pattern of the future butterfly. After another day or two, the final transformation occurs. The pupa splits and the butterfly creeps out which, in its turn, hangs down from the twig to dry. In twenty minutes or so he's ready to fly. In a flow of sunshine, the butterfly sees the world. What had been hope comes to fruition.

For our hope to come to fruition, it looks for the good in people, including ourselves, instead of harping on the worst. Hope opens doors where despair closes them; hope discovers what can be done instead of grumbling about what can't; hope regards problems, small or large, as opportunities; hope cherishes no illusions, but doesn't yield to cynicism; hope sets big goals and isn't frustrated by small setbacks; hope puts up with modest gains, realizing that "the longest journey starts with one step"; hope accepts misunderstandings as the price for serving others; and hope is a good loser because it has the divine assurance of final victory.

Scriptural hope isn't just optimism or only "thinking positive thoughts." It's much more. Optimism is based on observation and positive possibilities in the external world. Biblical hope finds no such assurance. It doesn't promise that our projects will succeed or that we will find within ourselves the capacity to overcome all obstacles. Biblical hope is bluntly realistic. Its roots in Scripture are full of stories about evil, sin, domination, war, pain, and failure. It meets these with a relentless insistence that God is bringing a new creation to birth. Despite all visible evidence, despite discouragement, hurt, and exhaustion, despite our limitations and the smallness of our efforts, God is at work.

It's in God's being there that the profound mystery and transformative power of biblical hope lies. Our hope is engendered in the midst of suffering. Instead of glossing over the pain, it goes straight to the heart, saying, "Precisely here in these circumstances is where we must be hopeful." Such hope rooted in the promise of things we don't see is a gift from God and can't be self-generated. We accept that gift only when we're able to relinquish our own versions of expectation, outcome, success, and control. The cornerstone of hope lies in Jesus' resurrection where, unexpectedly and seemingly impossibly, life defeats death.

So, in the midst of difficulty and hard times, we persevere in hope. A hope that is creative. A hope that engenders action. A hope that gives room for forgiving.

Man's way leads to a hopeless end; God's way leads to an endless hope! Hope for our greater conversion to God this Lent will make a happier celebration of Easter!

Pray and Act Boldly

Today's first reading is the only excerpt from the Book of Esther in all the liturgy. The story of Esther is unique in several ways. It's not written for the purpose of setting forth any important moral or religious ideal. It's a story of a Jewish maiden named Esther who was made queen in the court of the Persian king Ahasuerus and who was instrumental in the defeat of a plot which was intended to bring about a wholesale slaughter of the Jewish people.

While there may be some basis in history for these events, the details can't be regarded as historical fact. It's illustrative of the spirit of Jewish nationalism, a patriotic rather than a religious story. Its admission to the canon of Sacred Scripture is believed to be due primarily to the fact that it contains an account of the origin of the feast of Purim. There is no evidence among Persian records of a Jewish maiden becoming a queen in a Persian court. But historical accuracy wasn't the purpose of the story; it was designed to illustrate the antagonism between foreign nations and the Jews. Esther's decision to risk her life in order to save her people from the plot to kill them is the noblest point of the story.

The story opens with an account of a seven-day royal Persian feast. On the last day the king asks his queen, Vashti, to display her royal beauty before the guests. She refuses, and the king becomes so angry that he issues a decree that a new queen shall reign in her place. He therefore orders that beautiful maidens be brought to his court from various parts of his realm; from these, he shall select one as the new queen. A Jew named Mordecai presents his beautiful niece Esther. He takes special care not to reveal that she is a Jewess. After Esther is made queen, Mordecai learns of a plot being made against the king's life. He reports it to Esther, who in turn makes it known to the king, and the plotters are put to death.

Meanwhile, a man named Haman has been promoted to a very high place in the government and promulgates orders that whenever he passes by, people must bow to him. Mordecai, because of his Jewish qualms, refuses. This makes Haman angry; he persuades the king to pass a decree that on a certain day all of the Jews are to be slaughtered. Mordecai pleads with Esther to intercede in their behalf with the king. It's a dangerous mission for her, but she risks her life to carry it out. Haman, on the other hand, is delighted that the king has issued the decree, and in anticipation of the slaughter he constructs a gallows on which Mordecai is to be hung.

During the night, when the king is unable to sleep, he gives orders to his servants to read to him from the official records. They come across the account of the plot against the king's life which had been revealed by Mordecai. When the king finds that nothing has been done to honor the man who had saved his life, he begins to wonder about an appropriate reward.

Seeing Haman outside, the king calls him in and asks what should be done for one "whom the king delights to honor." Haman, supposing that he's the one, suggests a series of elaborate things. When he has finished, the king orders that all these shall be done to honor Mordecai. On the day which had been appointed for the slaughter of the Jews, the decree is reversed and the Jews are encouraged to slaughter their enemies.

The Book of Esther is concrete proof that prayer isn't as simple as it may seem. Queen Esther prayed to God for help and courage in a time of great national crisis. But she did a lot more than pray: She took God's help in her own hands. She had the winning combination of sincere prayer and her own work — as in that old saying, "Pray as though everything depends on God; work as though everything depends on you."

Does Jesus, in contrast, make prayer sound too easy? Is

prayer according to him like those cash machines where we in-
sert our plastic card and get money? Jesus isn't guaranteeing that
the *exact* object of every prayer will be granted as asked — but
only that God will hear our prayer and give us what's best for
us. That, after all, is the way it was with him: His condemnation
as a sinner, his unjust trial, and his cruel death show that not
every prayer is answered as asked. But instead of rescue he received resurrection, which is better.

Lastly in today's gospel excerpt, Jesus enunciates the Golden
Rule: "Do to others as you would have them do to you" (v. 31).
This isn't a *quid pro quo* ethic, whereby one who receives good is
obliged to reciprocate. And, rather than being *reactive*, whereby
we do good for people who have previously done good for us,
it's *pro-active*, whereby we do good for people who have *not* done
good for us, and from whom we don't expect good in return. Pro-
active love is fundamental to Christian living.

Some may be surprised to learn that the Golden Rule is a
heartpiece of other religions, too. Buddhism says, "Hurt not others in ways that you yourself would find hurtful" (*Udana-Varga*
5,18). Confucius, the Chinese philosopher about 500 years before Christ, said, "Do not unto others what you would not have
them do unto you" (*Analects* 15,23). Hinduism says, "do naught
unto others which would cause you pain if done to you"
(*Mahabharata* 5,1517). Taoism says, "Regard your neighbor's
gain as your own, and your neighbor's loss as your own loss" (*Tai
Shang Kan Ying P'ien*). Islam says, "No one of you is a believer
until he desires for his brother that which he desires for himself" (*Sunnah*). The Jewish *Talmud* says, "What is hateful to you,
do not to your fellow man" (*Shabbat* 32id).

It's also in Socrates, the Greek philosopher, about 400 years
before Christ; in the early Stoic philosophers of Greece and Rome,
beginning about 300 years before Christ; in the Book of Tobit
(4:15), about 200 years before Christ; in Hillel, one of the great
Jewish rabbis, who was born shortly before Christ; and in Philo,

the Jewish thinker from Alexandria in Egypt who lived roughly the same time as Jesus. But *Jesus* is *unique* in teaching that "others" includes everyone created by God, including enemies. God's creation didn't make anything without a purpose — though mosquitoes come close.

Friday, First Week of Lent
Ezk 18:21-28; Mt 5:20-26

Personal Responsibility
for Reconciliation

A cartoon shows passengers fleeing a sinking ship. As the survivors huddle together in a small lifeboat, their nightmare worsens as their boat springs a serious leak. One passenger remarks, "At least it's not *our* half that's leaking." But we have to remember that we're all in this boat of life together. That means that we have to take personal responsibility and live in charity with everybody around us.

The generation of the prophet Ezekiel felt that their troubles (the fall of their nation and their exile in Babylon, where they were now living) were a punishment for the sins of others, usually their ancestors. Ezekiel, the prophet of individual responsibility, rejected excuses as a cop-out. To support his position, he cited two cases. The first (v. 26) justifies the punishment of a wicked person. The second (v. 27f.) points out the rewards of a person who has turned from wickedness to goodness. In Ezekiel, "to die" and "to live" refer not so much to physical life as to the quality of life that stems from decisions made. His implication is that all of us have the responsibility to act with awareness of the consequences of our actions.

We don't realize how influential our actions are. For good or bad, we constantly influence people around us. There is no sin, not even the most intimate and secret one, the most strictly individual one, that exclusively concerns the person committing it. Most important are the *spiritual* effects of our actions. And for those, ever since Adam blamed Eve and Eve blamed the serpent, it seems part of human nature to want to "pass the buck." But for the making of our lives, the buck stops with each of us.

In today's context, all of it means a Lenten call to growth in maturity. This in turn means such interior qualities as the ability to control anger and settle differences without violence; patience, the willingness to pass up immediate pleasure in favor of long-term gain; perseverance, the ability to stick with a situation in spite of discouraging setbacks; the capacity to face unpleasantness, discomfort, and defeat without collapse; the bigness to say "I was wrong" when we were wrong and, when we were right, resisting the satisfaction of saying, "I told you so"; the ability to make a decision and follow it through. It also means coming through in a crisis. And it's the art of living in peace with what we can't change, the courage to change what we know should be changed, and the wisdom to know the difference between them.

Jesus, after pointing out the correct spirit of the Mosaic Law, gives four out of many possible examples of where his way of life demands personal responsibility: anger, adultery, divorce, and oaths. In today's gospel, he speaks of the first, anger. Jesus says that the commandment against the sin of murder is a command against anger (v. 22): the cancerous *cause*, and not merely the *effect*.

Anger, as with all emotions, is neither good nor bad. It's helpful to understand how we experience anger and how we respond to it. First, anger is experienced in our body, thoughts, moods, and behavior. When we're angry we often breathe harder, our heart beats faster, and we may feel pain or tightness in our stomach, head, back, or chest. With it we may also feel sad, anxious, agitated, or frightened, and we might scream, strike out aggressively, run away, freeze, or withdraw into silence. We can exacerbate it all by the choices we make. By examining and understanding how we deal with anger, we can make better choices. One who angers us controls us!

Jesus is both a good psychologist and a good theologian. He realized what modern psychology is more and more discovering: that for the avoidance of heart attacks and for overall good psychical health, we have to heal the basic *attitude*. Theologically, the sinfulness of the deeper attitude has the potential for manifesting itself in many acts unless it's recognized and brought to the Savior. When that happens, the act of sin can become a *felix culpa*, a happy fault, drawing awareness to the underlying attitude of alienation.

To the degrees of anger, extending even to thoughts, there are corresponding degrees of responsibility. Both Peter and Judas were guilty of denial and betrayal. Peter had an attitude of trust and therefore surrender. Judas, on the other hand, had an attitude of brooding anger. This in turn led to his flight from Jesus and his destruction.

Not only must we pardon those who have offended us; we must be the *first to seek* reconciliation even when the fault is on the other side (v. 23f.). Jesus says it's impossible to engage in worship, which is closely related to reconciliation with God, until we're at peace with our neighbor. He also recommends what today's lawyers advise: the settling of disagreements equitably out of court. To concede today may be the best way to succeed tomorrow. Jesus is saying: Be open to talking, to listening, to risking change in our human relationships; how else can we be converted in our relationships with God?

Our Lenten penances must be accompanied by charity.

Some of the best penances are those which refer to love for other people: for example, knowing how to say "sorry" when we've offended someone; making the sacrifices involved in forming another soul — a youth, perhaps — for whom we're responsible; exercising patience; seeing the need to forgive promptly and generously; giving alms; not complaining about those who have done us some harm; deeds of understanding others, and of courtesy, generosity, and mercy.

A single act of reconciliation with God and other human beings — an appropriate object for Lent — can be the most difficult thing we do during this season of grace. That one effort can be more demanding than any amount of fasting or other self-denial.

The people to whom Ezekiel spoke were no different from us. Students blame their teachers for bad grades, teachers their students for not working hard enough; wives blame their husbands for family problems, husbands their wives; parents blame their children, children their parents; Catholics blame "the Church" for all sorts of things, unmindful that if our Church were perfect, we probably couldn't belong. And like children who constantly complain that someone or something isn't "fair," we complain that life isn't fair, and that even God isn't fair. And it's true: God isn't fair. Good that He isn't. If He were, we'd all be in trouble.

Reach Out

By this time, we've considered basic Lenten practices: prayer, fasting, repentance. Today's gospel makes us realize a major roadblock in our journey: the command to love our enemies. Our enemies are people who are malicious, intend to harm us, harass us, stalk us, oppress us, and in general make our life miserable. Most of us have probably never had a no-holds-barred enemy. But what Jesus expects is that we do a better job loving those people with whom we don't get along. While they don't want to kill us they do sometimes try our patience.

It's hard for us to realize the truth of Jesus' saying that his listeners had heard it said that they should hate their enemy (v. 43f.). But the legitimacy of hating enemies was *precisely* what they had been taught. Regarding a *rasha*, for the hopelessly wicked, the Talmud clearly states: *mitzvah lisnoso* — one is obligated to hate him.

The view of the Mishnah, set down at about the time Paul wrote his Letter to the Romans, explicitly singled out specific wicked men in biblical history who would never be saved. Jewish intolerance for the wicked is confirmed in the much later interpretation of damnation by the great Jewish philosopher Moses Maimonides (A.D. 1135-1204). In his view, souls are never eternally punished in hell: The presence of the truly wicked is so intolerable to the Almighty that they never even experience an afterlife. Rather, at death they just disappear.

The Jewish Scriptures — the "Old Testament" — provide many examples of hatred and revenge against enemies as being the constant teaching of the ancients. Consider a few. The Philistines seized Samson and gouged out his eyes. When they brought him to Gaza and bound him, Samson convinced an attendant to put him between two supporting pillars of the temple. He prayed for strength that for his two eyes he might avenge himself on the Philistines. He grasped the two columns, pushed hard, and killed at his death more than those he had killed during his lifetime (Jg 16:28-30). Samson's rage taught that hate can be virtuous when one is dealing with the frightfully wicked. Rather than forgive, we can wish ill; rather than hope for repentance, we can instead hope that our enemies experience the wrath of God.

Even prophets were sometimes infected with the theology of hatred. Jonah, when told by God to preach repentance at Nineveh, showed an intolerant nationalism which limited the mercy of God to His own people. He fled from his God-appointed mission to the cruel Ninevites, which he found very distasteful (Jon 1:2ff.). And the great Samuel, having come upon the Amalekite king Agag, after Agag was already captured and the Amalekites exterminated, responded in anger: "'Bring Agag... here to me.'... And he cut Agag down" (1 S 15).

Every bloody detail is recounted in Deborah's ebullient song about the woman Jael, who killed Sisera, the Canaanite general who had oppressed the Israelites for twenty years: "With her left hand she reached for the peg, with her right, for the workman's mallet. She smashed into [the sleeping Sisera's] temple with the peg. At her feet he sank down, fell, lay still.... May your enemies perish thus, O Lord!" (Jg 5:26-31).

In refusing to forgive their enemies, Jewish leaders sought not merely their defeat, but their disgrace. When Queen Esther had already had Haman hanged (Est 7:10) — the Hitler of his time, attempted exterminator of the Jewish people — the Jew Mordecai had himself authorized by royal decree "to kill, destroy, wipe out, along with their wives and children, every armed group... which should attack them, and to seize their goods as spoil" (Est 8:11). "The Jews... did to their enemies as they pleased" (Est 9:5). Not satisfied with that, Esther asked King

Ahasuerus that the already dead ten sons of Haman be hanged on gibbets, and the king acquiesced (Est 9:13).

With all this as background, it's easy to understand the venomous hatred with which the adulteress Herodias and her young daughter Salome could demand of Herod Antipas the head of John the Baptist on a platter.

Jesus, in today's most radical section of his Sermon on the Mount, a passage presenting further applications of his basic principle that the holiness of his followers is to exceed that of the scribes and Pharisees — those who taught the Law of Moses! — said we're to *love* our *enemies*! Jews were taught to hate the wicked because they believed that God, too, despises the wicked. Jesus argues that God loves the wicked, and so must we.

Only if we love our enemies and expect nothing back will we be acting like God and in accord with Jesus' new teaching. When we've purified ourselves, by the grace of God, to the point at which we can truly love our enemies, a beautiful thing happens. It's as if the boundaries of the soul become so clean as to be transparent, and a unique light then shines forth. And, as God's conduct shows, there's nothing inconsistent between the Golden Rule and the Iron Rule, which — an aspect of "tough love" — is never to do for others what they can do for themselves. Difficult? Indeed it is. That's why G.K. Chesterton said, "Christianity has not been tried and found wanting; it has been found difficult and not tried."

The first thing we're called to do when we think of others as our enemies is to pray for them. Sometimes that isn't easy. But it's impossible to lift our enemies up in the presence of God and at the same time continue to hate them. Prayer converts the enemy into a friend and is thus the beginning of a new relationship. There is probably no prayer as powerful as this.

Unfortunately, hatred seems to be a basic instinct. We don't have to turn back to the Jewish Scriptures to find evidence for that: Our times give easy examples every day. But holiness —

which is not just otherworldly — precludes any spirit of enmity, revenge, and grudge-bearing.

Jesus sums it all up by saying that we should be perfect, just as our heavenly Father is perfect (v. 48). The definition of the perfection that God expects has been argued from the beginning. It isn't to be confused with the ancient Greek notion of perfection, which is to arrive at a moral peak point and become changeless. Through history, the perfectibility of people has meant many other possibilities: that we're capable of wholly subordinating ourselves to God's will; that we can attain to our natural end; that we can become like self-regulating machines.

Jesus' followers, of course, reject those naturalistic kinds of perfectionism. We see, as the apex of God's kind of perfection, compassion — a willingness to suffer with others — the object of which is always changing. Jesus practiced his own advice to love one's enemies. He called his betrayer, Judas, a friend and willingly offered himself to his executioners to whom Judas had handed him over. Those who love in Jesus's unconditional and non-selective way are true children of the God of limitless love.

Perhaps in the real world we can't act on this advice completely — for example, if we were a prisoner in a concentration camp with sadistic guards — but they are ideals. And it's good to remember how non-violence has triumphed in many situations in our world: in the civil rights cause in the '60's in the United States, for example, in the Philippines revolution in the '80's, and in the bloodless revolution which brought the collapse of the Soviet Union in the '90's. It's good to remember, too, that even pagans for their own reasons do good to those who are good to them. Machiavelli, for instance, advises that, when you do good, spread it out, so people won't forget; if, on the other hand, you should have to do evil, do it all at once, so that people might forget.

We Christians are called to go beyond justice; we're called to the heroic love of which Jesus speaks today.

Take an Honest Look Inside

There's a true story of young Mark who talked incessantly in the third grade of the Catholic school he attended. The Franciscan Sister who taught his class had to remind him again and again that talking without permission wasn't acceptable. What impressed her was that every time she corrected him for misbehaving, he said sincerely, "Thank you for correcting me, Sister!"

The Sister was transferred to teaching junior-high math, and she had young Mark in class again. He was more handsome than ever and just as polite. Because he had to listen carefully to the teacher's instructions in the "new math," he didn't talk as much as he had in the third grade. One Friday, the class had worked hard on a difficult new concept, and the students were frustrated and edgy. To stop the crankiness, the Sister asked everyone in the class to write down every student's name and also write the nicest thing they could think of about that person. As the students left the room, each one handed Sister the papers. Mark said, "Thank you for teaching us, Sister. Have a good weekend."

That Saturday, the Sister listed on a separate sheet of paper what everyone else had written about each individual. On Monday, she gave each student the list of what had been written about him or her. Before long, the entire class was smiling. The Sister heard repeated whispers, "I never knew that others liked me so much."

No one ever mentioned those papers in class again. The Sister never knew if the students ever discussed the papers after class or with their parents. But that didn't matter: The students were again happy with themselves and one another. They moved on.

Years later the Sister got word that Mark had died in Iraq. She was asked to attend the funeral, and she came. Most of Mark's

former classmates were also present. At Mark's coffin, the Sister
would have given anything if he could just talk to her. As she
stood at the grave after the funeral was over, Mark's mother and
father wanted to speak to her. His father said, "We want to show
you something," and, taking a wallet out of his pocket, he said,
"They found this on Mark when he was killed. We thought you
might recognize it." He carefully removed from the billfold two
pieces of note paper that had obviously been taped, folded, and
refolded many times. The Sister recognized the paper as the one
on which she had listed all the good things each of Mark's classmates had written about him.

"Thank you so much for doing that," Mark's mother said.
"As you can see, Mark treasured it." Mark's classmates gathered
around them; they all said that they still had their lists, too — in
the top drawer of a desk, in a wedding album, in a diary.

When they left, the Sister sat down and cried — for Mark,
for his friends who would never see him again, and for how special it was for people to tell one another that they love and care
about them, and that they have good qualities which are special
and important. She was thankful that her students had done it
before it was too late.

That class's injunction to note the positive qualities in others is a good rule of Lent and of life for all of us. Jesus advises us
in today's gospel to be compassionate, non-judgmental, non-con-
demning, forgiving of the faults we see, and generous in our as-
sessments of others. In some situations in life we can't escape
the obligation to make judgments even on the moral character
of others. Parents, fiancées, employers, civil judges, church ad-
ministrators, and the like, all have this obligation. Jesus' teaching warns, however, against usurping the definitive judgment of
God, who alone sees the heart. By contrast with God's judgment,
we must recognize our judging as tentative, partial, and inad-
equate.

There are, of course, many faults both in ourselves and others. In today's first reading, what a powerful public confession the prophet Daniel makes! He puts together not just peccadilloes, but a pile of terrible sins, wickedness, evil, rebellion, disobedience, and treachery. Daniel's earnest prayer isn't a prayer of an individual but of the community; and it's not a plea for enlightenment on the meaning of the not-yet-fulfilled prophecy of Jeremiah about the restoration of Israel after 70 years in exile, but an acknowledgment of public guilt and a supplication for the restoration of Zion.

God's superabundant response to the generosity of our good hearts is described in the picturesque image of one's lap not being able to contain His cascade of prizes (v. 38). His exchange of pardon for pardon is wonderfully pictured as overflowing: pressed down, shaken together, running over. How surprised and grateful would the Old Testament prophet Daniel be to hear Jesus' advice on generous assessment of an honest look into God and one another in today's gospel!

Tuesday, Second Week of Lent
Is 1:10,16-20; Mt 23:1-12

Wearing Overalls Rather than a Crown

In today's gospel, St. Matthew collects into one place many of Jesus' strong criticisms of the scribes and Pharisees — mainly two. One is the general strictness of their interpretations of the Law, a strictness which wasn't humane and which was at times criticized also by some rabbis. With their 613 rules and regulations,

the Pharisees were making religion an intolerable burden. If any
religion makes life depressing instead of full of joy, a hindrance
rather than a help, a weight to drag one down instead of wings
to lift one up, it's a menace to people.

Jesus' second criticism is of the religious leaders' vanity, conceit, and hypocrisy. There was no more hellish place on earth
than Berlin in late 1944 and the early months of 1945. Its people
were slowly starving to death in horrific conditions that included
a relentless bombing campaign by the Allied air forces. At Christmas, Berliners with a sense of humor were heard to quip: "Be
practical: Give a coffin."

Though he knew he had lost World War II, the vain Hitler
scorned any notion of surrender and the vain Stalin was obsessed
with the possibility that the Allies might beat the Soviets to Berlin. This resulted in unspeakable savagery. German women, rang-
ing from the very young to the elderly, were gang raped, muti-
lated, humiliated, and then frequently murdered by Red Army
soldiers. When one of the high Soviet generals — considered
intelligent and enlightened — was asked what he planned to do
to rein in the looting and destruction by his troops, he replied,
"It's now time for our soldiers to issue their own justice." In the
end, it was all senselessness which resulted from the outrageous
vanity of both Hitler and Stalin.

One thing that vanity and conceit caused the Pharisees to
do was to widen their phylacteries (v. 5). Phylacteries are little
boxes containing Scripture texts which Jews bind to their fore-
head and left wrist when saying their prayers. The Law had commanded them to keep the Law as a sign on their hand and as a
memorial between their eyes. They interpreted this literally instead of figuratively, the sense in which the regulation was probably meant. There was nothing wrong with that, except their
widening their phylacteries in order that everyone would see
them. They were not unlike moderns who put all kinds of signs
on their car: medallions of their memberships on their wind-

shields, statues of saints on their dashboard, police connections on their rear windows.

The Pharisees also lengthened their tassels. Originally these were to be worn on the four corners of their cloak as reminders of the Law. The Pharisees enlarged them out of ostentation. And they coveted places of honor at banquets (v. 6) and the front seats of honor in synagogues. The back seats were assigned to children and the unimportant; the further front the seat, the greater the honor. The most honored seats of all were those that *faced* the congregation: If you were seated there, people could see that you were present, and you could act piously to impress them.

They also loved greetings in marketplaces (v. 7). Though courtesy demands that marks of respect be given proportionate to the dignity of a person, to seek greetings was a self-serving status symbol. And they were fond of the salutation "Rabbi," which meant "My master" — a teacher of the Law of Moses. This title was often a flattering term of address for Jesus in the gospels, sometimes as a sly introduction to a nasty question.

Jesus rejects three honorary titles (vv. 8-12): master, father, and teacher. This prohibition must be understood in its context; if it were taken literally, it would mean that we shouldn't call our physician "doctor," because that word means "learned one," or anyone "mister" because that means master and ultimately comes from "magister" or teacher, or our physical father "father" or our spiritual father, the priest, "father." What Jesus forbids is for Christians to use titles for mere ostentation, arrogance, or pomposity. He also wants to nudge people not to use these terms in a childish way that is unable to question authority. All must acknowledge that any "fatherhood" that one might have is in God, from whose heavenly Fatherhood the authority of earthly fatherhood derives.

Jesus then repeats what he had said elsewhere: "Whoever exalts himself will be humbled, but whoever humbles himself will be exalted" (v. 12). A modern way of saying that is, "It's better to sit in the back row and be discovered than to sit in the front row and be found out." As St. Augustine put it, there's something in humility that exalts the mind and something in exaltation that abases it. Humility makes the mind subject to what is superior — ultimately, God. Exaltation, on the other hand, spurns subjection to *any*thing, even what is superior.

There's nothing wrong with ambition. Jesus simply turns ambition around: ambition to serve instead of for personal gain, to do things for others instead of having them do for us. To have the ambition to be the last one of all doesn't mean, however, being apathetic. With Christians, if they let people see their good deeds, it's for the purpose of glorifying our heavenly Father.

There are lessons in today's liturgy for both the Church at large and for each member. As for the Church, wherever it becomes strong because of persecution as in Poland, or looked up to for having fought for human rights as in Central and South America, or respected because of history as in Ireland, there's a danger that the Church may use power incorrectly. Adding to Lord Acton's dictum that "power corrupts, and absolute power corrupts absolutely," Nietzsche observed that "power makes stupid."

As for every Church member, Jewish leaders of Jesus' time were not then, nor are they now, the only ones who perform their works to be seen, demand places of honor at public functions, expect public marks of respect, or relish honorific titles. Very few hierarchical organizations are able to withstand the lure of decorations to mark out various ranks. Napoleon is quoted as saying, "Men are led by such baubles."

Vanity — by way of flattery — is well illustrated by Aesop's fable of the fox and the crow. The crow flew to a tree with a stolen piece of meat in her beak. A fox, who saw her, wanted the meat, so he looked up into the tree and said, "How beautiful you are, my friend! Your feathers are fairer than the dove's. Is your voice as beautiful? If so, you must be the queen of birds." The crow was so happy in his praise that she opened her mouth to show how she could sing. Down fell the piece of meat. The fox seized upon it and ran away. The usual moral is *avoid falling for flattery*, but some people take the story to mean *flattery will get you everything*.

In our time, vanity would be applicable to the young lady of sixteen conceitedly preening before a mirror whose father reminded her: "You can take no credit for beauty at sixteen. But if you're beautiful at 60, it will be your own soul's doing. Then and then alone you may be proud of it and be loved for it." Equally interesting is the woman who, aiming to prove her contention that men are vainer than women, said in a speech: "It's a pity that the most intelligent and learned men attach least importance to the way they dress. Why, right in this room the most cultivated man is wearing the most clumsily knotted tie!" As if on a signal, every man in the room immediately put his hand to his tie to straighten it.

One final example is the notoriously self-centered comedian who was due to be the Guest of Honor at a show business dinner. In the men's room before the affair, he stood in front of the mirror adjusting his tie, pinching his cheeks to heighten their color, and checking out his appearance in general. Then he asked the attendant, "How many really important men do you think there are in the banquet hall tonight?" The attendant said, "One less than you think."

Every Christian, despite the temptations to Pharisaism in all of us, is to seek to render selfless service rather than to obtain titles, recognition, or power. The best soil for the growth of Christian virtue is humble service and detachment: detachment not only from things, but from praise and prestige. In the humble Christ — poor, shunned, and oppressed — is where the growth of virtue always finds fertile soil.

Greatness Is Service

After a forest fire in Yellowstone National Park, a forest ranger found a bird literally petrified in ashes, perched statuesquely on the ground at the base of a tree. The ranger touched the bird with a stick. At that, three tiny chicks scurried from under their dead mother's wings. The loving mother, keenly aware of the impending disaster, had carried her offspring to the base of the tree and had gathered them under her wings, instinctively knowing that the toxic smoke would rise and kill. She could have flown to safety, but had refused to abandon her babies, remaining steadfast even when the blaze had scorched her tiny body.

Although that mother bird's example of lack of selfish ambition and a sole desire to be of service to her chicks was only in the animal kingdom, she nevertheless gives human beings something to think about with regard to proper ambition. When is ambition valid? Certainly when it's needed for our self-respect, or to get us moving, or when support of our loved ones is at stake. We all have hopes, aims, and desires, and need proper ambition to motivate us to fulfill them. Ambition is never ethical, however, when it's connected with ruthlessness, as in today's first reading, or with insensitivity, as in today's gospel.

In the words of Jeremiah, the passionate and persecuted prophet who lived some 600 years before Jesus, we get a foretaste of Jesus' final days. Jeremiah's difficult time of dedicated preaching brought from his people refusal to repent, betrayal, the threat of death, arrest, and imprisonment. Jeremiah discovered that his enemies were plotting to kill him, even though he had done them only good. It was another display of the mystery of bad things happening to good people.

Today's gospel begins with Jesus' third prediction — the

most detailed of all — of his betrayal, death, and resurrection. Jesus the resolute leader wanted to encourage his Apostles beforehand with words he craved for them to remember afterwards. His advice — to be the servants and the last of all — isn't easy to accept and put into practice.

Evidently, the Zebedee family didn't understand Jesus' teaching on the Kingdom of God. In what looks like a family affair, Salome, the mother of James and John, placed before Jesus their ambition to occupy his highest two places of honor. To sit at the right hand of a king meant to have the highest place; the place at his left hand was the next best. Their timing, right after Jesus' detailed forecast of his death, was shockingly insensitive and its demand outrageous.

Although St. Mark's gospel has the sons themselves approaching Jesus, St. Matthew is probably more exact in having the mother Salome make the request. Perhaps they thought it would look less self-interested that way, or they had more reliance on her feminine powers of persuasion. Their petition was dramatic: they declared themselves ready to risk death with Jesus — provided, of course, that he guarantee them his kingdom's most powerful positions.

With the utmost patience Jesus told Salome she didn't know what she was asking. He asked her sons bluntly if they could withstand the same painful heartache as his. Envisioning a great royal court that they associated with the Messiah, they brashly said they could. Unwittingly, they were to live up to that promise. About twelve years after Jesus' death, James would be the first of the Apostles to suffer martyrdom (Ac 12:2): he was beheaded in Jerusalem. Later John, the only Apostle to die a natural death, was, according to Tertullian, put into a cauldron of boiling oil; miraculously escaping, he was scourged and afterwards exiled to Patmos (Rv 1:9), where he eventually died.

So from a spiritual point of view their prayer was answered in a better way than they expected. The closer one imitates Jesus' spirit of self-sacrifice in the service of others, the greater one's position in heaven. Spiritual suffering can take many forms: recognizing our personal limitations in not being able to do or be everything we would like, for example, or dull routine, or an inability to reach certain people, or frustration over our personal improvement not being as easy as self-help books make it look.

The other Apostles became indignant at James and John — unfortunately, not out of disappointment over their ambition. The gospels show elsewhere that they had similar ambitions. But James and John had got there first. Our earliest impressions of the first disciples in their beginnings are usually more positive than is justified. In today's gospel, we see the human reality. We may wonder if the Apostles had become less indignant later as they watched Salome hold her ground with the other women at the foot of Jesus' cross while the Apostles themselves, along with others, all ran for their lives. Spare us, O Lord, from the jealousy of religious people!

So now Jesus called them all together for a much-needed lesson on ambition. He had often declared that he must suffer and die; now, in his final words in this passage, he explained that he accepts death for the salvation of all humankind. Uncontrolled ambition was put to shame, and sensitive fraternal charity came to life.

Famed psychiatrist Dr. Karl Menninger once gave a lecture on mental health, after which someone from the audience asked him what he would suggest that a person do in the event of a suspected impending nervous breakdown. Everyone thought that Dr. Menninger would advise as a preventive measure a visit to a psychiatrist. Instead, he replied: "Lock up your house, go to the other side of the railroad tracks, and find people in need. Then do something to help. Immerse yourself in the lives of others." That's a sure cure for a nervous breakdown, for boredom, and for a whole host of other vexations.

And there are stories of soldiers in combat who have vol-

untarily fallen on a hand grenade, their body absorbing the blast
and the fragments to protect their comrades. Numerous medical personnel and chaplains have stayed behind with the
wounded, only to be captured or even killed by the enemy. Some,
like Father Maximilian Kolbe, have been declared saints. In a concentration camp he voluntarily took the place of a condemned
man to die a slow death: the other man had a family dependent
on him.

For God, success is judged not by how much we can get
out of life, but how much we put into it. To aspire to greatness
is to aspire to lowliness. Even on a parish level, volunteers must
be wary lest they imitate pagan ambition, and must escape the
desire to be important in the same way that people want to be
important in a corporation; we must avoid our service being an
ego trip.

Thursday, Second Week of Lent
Jr 17:5-10; Lk 16:19-31

Compassionate Self-Giving

Jeremiah in today's first reading sets forth two possible directions
for the journey of the heart, which is the "seat of moral personality" (*Catechism of the Catholic Church*, #2517). Like Jesus,
Jeremiah gives his message twice over: in the language of a curse
and in the language of a blessing. And like Jesus, he states his
values in the present tense, meaning *now*: Blessed *is* the one who
trusts in the Lord, and cursed *is* the one whose heart turns away
from the Lord.

Jeremiah compares those who draw their life's inspiration

from God to a tree near the river's edge, whose roots drink in the life-giving water. He compares those who trust only in humankind to a barren bush in the desert, growing in a lava waste, a salt and empty earth (v. 6). In Jeremiah's time and in his parched land, where a person was always in danger of starvation because of drought, his metaphors were especially meaningful.

Jeremiah's tree by flowing waters grew little by little, while the bush in the desert, being shallow, gave up. The righteous person is wise enough to seek good models for his life, smart enough to avoid what may lead him to spiritual death, and insightful enough to use the opportunities of grace. The person whose hope is anywhere but in the Lord is insolent and unconcerned about sin.

Today's Responsorial Psalm continues the message: "Happy are they who hope in the Lord." In today's gospel, Jesus addresses those among the Pharisees "who loved money." He tells them — and us — the story of two men: Lazarus, the poor man, whose Hebrew name means "God is my help," and Dives, from the Latin adjective meaning "rich" — one of the "beautiful people" who went "first class" all the way.

Dives's flagrantly expensive outer garments were dyed in a purple that came from shells on the beaches of Tyre, so cherished that the veil of the Temple was made from it, and from time to time attempts were made to reserve it exclusively for the togas of the Roman emperor. At a time when the poor and hard-working populace were lucky if they got the cheapest cut of meat once a week, Dives dined sumptuously *every day* (v. 19).

There are still today many luxuries along the lines of Dives's life. Shops on Rodeo Drive in Los Angeles, Fifth Avenue in New York, the Via Veneto in Rome, the Champs Elysée in Paris, the Kufurstendam in Berlin. Extravagant hotels in Las Vegas. The indulgence of the "I'm worth it!" ads.

At the gate to Dives's palace lay Lazarus the beggar (v. 20) — right off the sidewalks of any modern city, where he lies in his cardboard shelter against the cold winds. He longed to eat the scraps (v. 21) from Dives's table. Lazarus wasn't only poor, but helpless — so helpless that hungry dogs licked his sores, and he didn't have the strength to chase them away!

Then death came. Lazarus was taken to heaven as a reward — not for his poverty, but for his trust in God. Dives went to a place of terrible torment (v. 23), where he was wracked with hunger and thirst.

Dives's torment wasn't because of molesting Lazarus in any way: He didn't. In a sense, he did nothing — but he did nothing about the rights of the poor. He was condemned not because luxury is evil, which it isn't, but because of apathy. Dives-types — his five brothers (v. 28) — continue to roam the earth, looking at the world's misery but not feeling it, and seeing without involvement fellow human beings in pain.

The urge for heaven is universal. For millennia, people have been asking the same questions about heaven: Do we keep our bodies? Are we reunited with loved ones? Can we eat, drink, make love? How do we get there? Who is in hell, or how many? The Church has never declared that any person — not even Judas — has damned himself. (By contrast, the Church has declared thousands of people to be saints and therefore in heaven.)

Heaven is the home of the one God, who is just and merciful, and heaven is a perfect place. In heaven, we live forever. Most people think about heaven in terms of what they want. That's why dog-lovers think they'll be reunited with their pets in heaven, and the exploited think of heaven as a place where they'll never have to work.

Early Jews believed that dead people, good and bad, all descended to the same destination, a nondescript underworld called *Sheol*. *Sheol* is a place of silence. There's nothing about it to fear, but nothing to look forward to, either: "The dead know nothing and they have no reward" (Ec 9:5). Some Jewish sages have concluded that the wicked perish in the grave; only the righteous will be resurrected to eternal life when the Messiah comes. However, the here and now is what matters for Jews, not the hereafter.

Through the years, Christian details of heaven were painted in as society evolved. Thomas Aquinas thought of it as a brilliant place, full of light and knowledge. Dante's *Divine Comedy* pictures heaven as a series of concentric spheres, with God in the center as a brilliant light; how close you get to God depends on your capacity for love and joy.

Jesus' story of Dives and Lazarus suggests that we need to think of hell as well as heaven. The most famous sermon in United States history was a graphic description of the horrors of hell. As Jonathan Edwards on July 16, 1741, expanded on his subject, "Sinners in the Hands of an Angry God," so many moans and cries rose from his proper New England congregation that he had to pause while his listeners recoiled in fear of their fate in the life to come.

Thoughts of hell began to fade, at least among liberal Protestants, during the nineteenth century. By the end of the twentieth century, it was a doctrine that most Christians cheerfully ignored. Today, few Catholics line up on Saturday nights to confess their sins, even mortal ones.

Ironically, hell has always been more exciting than heaven. The impact of Dante's *Inferno* changed the very language. The word *inferno* derives from the Latin word *inferus*, which means below or underneath. But because of *The Divine Comedy's* popular impact — and only because of it — the word *inferno* eventually took on the meaning of hell. There are far more English translations of Dante's *Inferno* than there are of his *Purgatorio* or *Paradiso*.

Milton in the seventeenth century more or less completed the imagery of hell when he wrote *Paradise Lost*, furnishing it with dungeons, fiery deluges, burning sulfur and, of course, awful devils and demons. Readers still thrill to the hell in Milton's *Para-*

dise Lost, where Satan is the chief person of the drama, but fewer people read about heaven in his *Paradise Regained.*

Christianity has traditionally affirmed that at death each individual is judged and ultimately consigned to heaven or hell. "If what we do now is to make no difference in the end," argued the philosopher Ludwig Wittgenstein, "then all the seriousness of life is done away with." The worst punishment of hell, rather than being an eternal torture chamber of fire and brimstone, is eternal separation from God — from all that is good, hopeful, and loving in the world. And this condition is chosen by the damned themselves, the ultimate exercise of their free will, not a punishment engineered by God.

Yet, of nearly 4,000 verses in the Gospels, Jesus speaks of hell in Mark only once, in Luke three times, in Matthew six times, in John not at all. He speaks of judgment in Mark only once, in Luke twice, in Matthew and John six times each. In his lengthiest consideration of judgment (Mt 25:31-46), his crucial question pivots on the issue of one's sensitivity to the suffering of the likes of the hungry, the thirsty, the imprisoned. If we contrast the relative rareness of Jesus speaking about hell or judgment with the profusion of times in the gospels when he both spoke and acted as one who has come to heal and forgive, we come away with a picture of Christian moral practice far different from what many Christians expect.

Whereas heaven is a gift, the existence of hell is the great compliment God pays to human beings. That's because we're creatures who can say no to God, and God will respect our wishes. He thinks that highly of us.

In hell, the arrogant Dives doesn't change! "As we live, so shall we die," is frightening but true. The tongue that had tasted the finest wines now longed for a drop of water and demanded that the saintly Lazarus — whose identity he knows exactly, even though he had never taken him in in his days and nights of need — be sent as his errand-boy to slake his thirst (v. 24)! When that didn't work, his boldness persisted, but now he begged — begged this time — for Lazarus to go as a messenger to his five brothers. He brazenly wound up pointing out to Abraham that if someone from the dead were to go to his brothers they would repent.

Abraham's answer to Dives's pleas were the equivalent of those saddest of words, "Too late! Too late!" Wondrous events — a voice from the grave, even remembrance of Christ's resurrection from the dead (v. 31) — won't automatically save people.

Unfortunately, our society hasn't changed essentially from the time of Christ. We reward our entertainers with lavish bounty while resenting persons on welfare; we give golden parachutes to failed Chief Executive Officers and nothing to workers laid off as a result of the CEOs' mistakes. Our society gives millions of dollars a year to corporate heads of clothing companies that pay fifty cents an hour to poor women who make the clothing.

. "Wealthfare" — the money our government hands out to corporations and wealthy individuals — presently amounts to three-and-a-half times more than the money spent on welfare for the poor; a mere reduction of wealthfare by 26 percent would eliminate our federal deficit. Even more shocking, some experts estimate that 11 years of government perks to the rich amount to more than the entire federal debt accumulated by the United States since the founding of this nation more than 200 years ago.

Where do *we* stand, both with regard to our government's policies and our personal attitudes toward the poor? Will Christ find us among the *complacent* rich? Hand-in-hand with wealth and power must go responsibility. If we have no sense of responsibility or concern for others, there follows a blindness and coldness of heart. The question to be asked of us is not, "Are you rich or are you poor?", as if one or the other would make us morally better, but, "Do you care, or are you complacent?"

Christianity has been accused of a lack of enthusiasm for human development based on the belief that the lot of the poor will be improved in the *next* life. But to delay meeting human need is a travesty of the gospel. What we think and do has consequences, and eternal ones.

Today's gospel story is about the choice that each one has to make: warm compassion or freezing indifference. Lent gives us the grace to keep making compassion our choice. Today, there's a single-file lineup of Lazaruses that would stretch around the world at least ten times. Obviously, we can't help all of them by ourselves — but before this Lent is over, we should each of us choose at least one Lazarus to help as generously as we can.

Friday, Second Week of Lent

Gn 37:3f.,12f.,17-28; Mt 21:33-43, 45f.

Acting on Accurate
Perspectives on Life

Perspective is important. In a photograph, the same object can as easily be seen as a close-up of a pock-marked basketball or as a long shot of the surface of the moon. Cockroaches at their own eye level are as big and menacing as jackals. A motion-picture close-up of the striking of an ordinary kitchen match can look like a roaring eruption of a blast furnace.

One of the lessons that the liturgies of Lent try to teach is an accurate perspective to our lives. Some of them present personalities of the Old Testament who are types of Our Lord. In today's first reading we're given a perspective of the Old Testament Joseph, a figure of Jesus the Redeemer.

At his father's request, Joseph traveled a long way to find his brothers. He brought them food and good news of their father. At first his brothers, who hated and envied him for being their father's favorite, considered killing him. Later, they sold him as a slave, and as such he was taken to Egypt. Over the years he became a highly-positioned economic advisor to the Pharaoh. In a time of famine he was the savior of his brothers, against whom he held no grudge despite their ill-treatment of him. He became a savior of the tribes of Israel as well as of the people of Egypt.

Our Lord, too, was sent by his heavenly Father, after a long series of prophets, also to save. And the people rejected him in a way similar to Joseph's brothers rejecting him. Proper perspective tells us that the suffering rendered to Jesus by the Jewish leaders was almost nothing compared with what we Christians make him undergo by our sins.

To help us in gaining perspective on sin, Lent is an opportune time. On the approach we adopt toward deliberate small sins will depend the progress we make in our interior life. Casual acceptance of these sins makes the soul insensitive to the inspirations of the Holy Spirit. These sins weaken the life of grace, make the virtues more difficult to practice, increasingly distance our soul from God, and lessen our capacity for interest in others.

Jesus had now been about his heavenly Father's business long enough to have acquired some of the smug Pharisees as his irremediable enemies. By now he knew that their murdering him was certain just as soon as they could get their plot in order. Yet his perspective on life was such that he had an inner peace. How did he handle his reverses? Well, on this occasion he told a story.

It's a story about God and the human race, and uses a metaphor to describe that relationship. Among the Bible's many metaphors to describe God's relationship with His people was the metaphor of the vineyard, from the "Song of the Vineyard" in Isaiah: a "divine love-song" in which God sees His people as His own vineyard, into which God has put great effort. From the Book of Genesis at the beginning of the Bible to the Book of Revelation at its end, the symbol of the vineyard is mentioned over a hundred times. The vineyard was also depicted in the golden vines decorating the entrance to the Temple.

Jesus, his death drawing nearer, was aiming at the smugness of the leaders of Israel, and drew attention to himself more boldly than before. He referred to himself as the keystone of the entire structure of the relations between God and the human race.

Jesus' audience had no way yet of knowing his surprise climax to this perspective, which was that *they*, the religious leaders and their followers with whom he was now coming in contact, were the ones who would drag him outside the city and put him to death. Part of the story too are *we*, the new Israel, the Church, God's vineyard now. At least as surprising is that God's vineyard would be given over to the poor and the outcasts. The last is because of God's *zaddiqah*: His integrity, uprightness, justice, and steadfast loyalty.

In the end there are two kinds of people: those good people who say to God, "Thy will be done," and those evil people to whom God says in their final condemnation, "Thy will be done."

If we think about our lives prayerfully, especially during Lent, we will gain perspective. We can't control the length of our life, but we can control its width and depth. We can't control the contour of our countenance, but we can control its expression. We can't control the weather, but we can control the atmosphere which surrounds us.

There were twin brothers in a small village. They grew up knowing nothing but poverty. Their father was an alcoholic and their mother a domestic worker. On their parents' way home one day, they were involved in a bus accident and died instantly. At age 17 the brothers were separated.

Years later, a family member decided to find them for a family reunion. One of the brothers, it was discovered, was a wealthy engineer who owned a construction company. He had a wife and three beautiful children. The other brother was an alcoholic with no sense of direction for his life.

The family member asked the engineer, "How did your life turn out like this?" He answered, "What did you expect with a childhood like mine?" She moved on to the other brother with the same question. His answer was, "What did you expect with a childhood like mine?"

People aren't disturbed by the things that happened, but by their perception of the things that happened and how they handled them.

Basketball or moonscape, cockroach or jackal, striking match or blast furnace, obstacle or instrument of growth in our lives depends on our perspective and what we do about it.

Saturday, Second Week of Lent
Mi 7:14f.,18-20; Lk 15:1-3, 11-32

Forgiveness of Ourselves and Others

A group of small boys at Sunday School listened intently as the teacher told them the parable of the Prodigal Son. After emphasizing the disagreeable attitude of the older brother, the teacher described the household's rejoicing at the return of the Prodigal Son.

"In the middle of the celebration, however," said the teacher, "there was one who failed to share in the festive spirit! Now, does anyone know who that was?"

Waving his hand frantically, one little boy said, "The fatted calf!"

If an Academy Award were given for Best Parable, the winner would be the parable of the Prodigal Son. The story has been so popular that it's often portrayed in the arts. George Balanchine choreographed it to a score by Prokofiev. Balanchine's Prodigal Son was an angry rebel against all ties. His leaps, done with great force, were signs of his rage, and when he pounded his fists against his body it was easy to imagine him shouting with defiance.

In a tavern scene, his reckless bravado failed when he realized that his drinking companions were treacherous. Robbed and battered by them, his body sagged and crumpled up. The way he crawled across the stage revealed his pain, exhaustion, and utter despair. The confident courtesan who tempted the Prodigal was simultaneously alluring in her gestures and aloof in her overall manner of emotional fire and ice.

Rembrandt did a famous painting on the parable of the Prodigal Son in which the father, who represents God, has a number of interesting features. First of all, he's depicted as blind. His eyes are shut and he sees the prodigal son not with his eyes but with his heart, to which he's tenderly holding the son's head. Moreover, he has one male hand (which is strongly pulling the wayward son to himself) and one female hand (which is softly caressing the son's back). Thus God is presented as both mother and father.

Rembrandt's painting invites us to see ourselves in each of its three characters — in the weakness of the wayward son, in the bitterness of the older brother, and in the compassion of the father/mother, God. We know that, like the younger son, we're often away from God because of our weaknesses. We know, too, that, like the older brother, we're often absent from the Father's love and celebration through our bitterness and anger. As we get older, we begin to realize that we may really be both sons.

But what Jesus' revelation in this parable really invites us to — powerfully evident in Rembrandt's painting — is to recognize in the Father his/her all-embracing, all-forgiving, caressing compassion. We're meant to radiate both God's masculine, fatherly embrace of the wayward, and God's feminine, motherly caress of the bitter. Thus God is both a blessing Father and caressing Mother who sees with the eyes of the heart.

The story in St. Luke's gospel began with the Pharisees' complaint that Jesus was eating with sinners. In truth, Jesus' dinner companions would never make the guest list at White House banquets or appear in society columns. And the Pharisees had a point. Whereas to us it may appear simply that Jesus was being friendly, in their culture sharing food together meant that the people at the table show that they accept one another. To counter the Pharisees, Jesus told three stories about God reaching out and about forgiveness. Because the three stories are of the lost — the lost sheep, the lost coin, and the lost son — some flippantly call this section the "Lost and Found Department."

After the first two stories' portrayal of God as one who *actively seeks* what is lost, Jesus told this glorious story of the Father who seems content to *wait* for a sinner to come to his senses and return home. The story might better be called "The Story of the Prodigal Father" — for "prodigal" means spendthrift, and it's indeed the Father who is spendthrift, lavishing His love, welcome, and forgiveness.

It's been said that the ingratitude of a child is more hurtful to a parent than the assassination attempt of a servant. What concerned this father most was that, whether he complied with his young son's heartless and callous request for his inheritance (v. 12) or not, he was going to lose his child.

Eventually, the son's misery brought him to his senses (v. 17). Here he was, this kosher boy, in a pig sty, envying the food of an animal that was itself not fit to be food. He had hit rock bottom. He determined — albeit selfishly — to rise and go to his father. The father's options with his returning son were many.

He could scold him.

But the father chose forgiveness.

Or he could demand an apology.
But the father chose forgiveness!
Or he could be condescendingly accepting.
But the father chose forgiveness!!
Or he could disown him.
But the father chose forgiveness!!!
Or he could demand that the son make restitution by making him work as a hired hand, which was what both the son and Jesus' audience expected.
But the father chose *forgiveness*!!!!

Now, there are many ways of forgiving. It's often done reluctantly, conveying continuing guilt to the recipient. Sometimes forgiveness is done in the form of a favor. Worse, at times the forgiver, in a form of blackmail, implies that the other's sin will still in some way be held over him. With *this* father, though, the forgiveness was *total,* offering to treat his son's sins as though they had never happened. And it was joyous: To celebrate it the father broke forth into typical Semitic poetry (v. 24). He threw his arms around his son, kissed him (v. 20), and instructed his servants to dress him as befits his son (v. 22): to give him a ring, a token of honor and authority, and sandals, the mark of a free man, since only slaves went barefoot. (The American slave's dream of heaven in the Afro-American spiritual is, "All God's chillun got shoes.")

The father had interrupted the younger son's prepared confession out of love; the elder son in turn interrupted the father's expression of forgiveness because of small-spiritedness. Part of his thinking was possibly that a piece of the money for this party might be coming out of his share of the estate! He complained about having done his duty (v. 29), and he undoubtedly had — but grimly. If over time his father hadn't heaped marks of affection upon him, it could well have been because his son's coldness made that impossible. The elder brother showed meanness of speech before the father in referring to his brother as "your son" (v. 30) rather than as "my brother." The father's answer was heart-rending: "My son, everything I have is yours" (v. 31).

The story has no ending. We don't know whether the elder brother goes into the house to join in the celebration, or whether he nurses his self-righteousness outside. There's no ending because it's not just a story: It's a challenge — to each one of us. If you're the prodigal son, will you come back? If you're the elder son, will you come in or stay outside? Can you follow the example of the loving forgiveness of the father?

In today's first reading the prophet Micah sets the eternal pattern for the prodigal son's father to follow. Sinners must be welcomed, wined, and dined, because that's the royal treatment God gives them. The original Father is the God who removes guilt, pardons sin, delights in clemency, has compassion, and casts all our sins into the depths of the sea.

When we talk about God as our Father, the kind of father we're talking about is one who loves us unconditionally, even though we make a real mess of things. Nothing speaks of the radical nature of God's love more than his teachings on forgiveness. Forgiveness is the final form of love, and *wholehearted* forgiveness is so loving that it's God-like.

Those realizations should inspire us to see our need for Jesus' gift of the sacrament of Reconciliation for God's forgiveness of our sins, saying, "I will rise and go to my Father."

And we're to imitate God's kind of love in our joyful forgiving of other people. In individual cases that may be difficult. To those who brood over injuries, it may be easier to learn Chinese than to say "I'm sorry" or "I forgive you." Even when we don't feel like forgiving, though, we must pray for the grace to do it. The very fact that we sincerely want to forgive means we've actually forgiven the person in our heart. Good feelings will follow, though not necessarily right away. Follow the advice of St. Augustine, who said: "Do what you can do, and pray for what you cannot yet do."

Remembering that forgiveness is humankind's deepest need and highest achievement, let's look into the far-away places where lost people (sometimes us!) tend to hide, and contribute to the healing forgiveness that we and our world so greatly crave.

Monday, Third Week of Lent

2 K 5:1-15; Lk 4:24-30

God Does the Unexpected

In view of the reputation of Jesus their native son, the people of Nazareth expected to be able to boast that one of their number was a miracle-worker. They believed that they had a right to demand that Jesus perform for them. Such was their total lack of faith and their hostility that not even Jesus could work a miracle there.

Although Jesus had to disagree with some of the things that were taught in the synagogue, he, unlike many modern Church critics, nevertheless faithfully attended the synagogue Sabbath services. Some members of Christ's Church ask many questions to attempt to justify their staying away. How can the Church, given certain bad aspects of her history, be seen as a privileged instrument of grace? Is God really to be found in an organization that slaughtered so many innocent people in the Crusades, used the Inquisition as a divine tool, sanctioned sexism for centuries, and has had religious wars, sinful silences, and blind imperialism? Is God really to be found in an organization that has some pedophiles among its ministers?

Yet no one can deny the good the Church has done. It has administered grace, produced saints, morally challenged the planet, and made, however imperfectly, a house for God to dwell in on this earth. To be connected with the Church identifies us with the finest persons of heroic soul within every time, country, race, and gender. To be a member of the Church is to carry the mantle of both the worst sins and the finest heroism.

Jesus had begun his sermon in today's gospel by stating his theme (v. 21): that that very day a Scripture passage from Isaiah was being fulfilled in their midst. Initially it didn't sink in that Jesus was talking about himself. The group listening to our Lord that day were, after all, many of the people who had known him when he was growing up: his teachers, the cobbler who repaired the family sandals, storekeepers who sold them food, childhood companions who ran with him through the town's streets and hills. They remembered the young boy who'd come to the synagogue with his parents.

Religion can be like a hometown: familiar, a constant in a chaotic world. Some people want to wrap religion around them like a security blanket, often to stay the same — and Jesus didn't provide that. Jesus was now (vv. 25-27) interpreting Scripture verses they probably knew by heart. He said that two of their favorite prophets, Elijah and Elisha, had worked many miracles among some non-Jews who received them and accepted them more favorably than some Jews did. The story of Naaman the Syrian leper to whom Jesus referred and whose story is told in our first reading today is delightful. Naaman, an army general of Syria, Israel's hostile northern neighbor, was handicapped at the height of his military career by a skin disease which at that time was called leprosy, but was apparently not bad enough to exempt him from his commission in the Syrian army.

Having tried every possible remedy without success, Naaman was sent by his king to seek a cure that was reported to be available from the Jewish prophet Elisha. Naaman came — with all his glittering, dignified, and mighty retinue — with a letter from his king to the king of Israel. He took along all kinds of expensive gifts: ten silver talents (each roughly a pound of silver), six thousand gold pieces, and ten festal garments. Naaman's approach scared the king of Israel out of his wits: He thought that the king of Syria was trying to say, "Cure my general Naaman or else!"

Elisha heard about his king's plight and asked that Naaman be sent to him. The king of Israel was glad to oblige. Humiliating though it was for the army commander of a great power to seek help in a vassal state from what appeared to be a religious eccentric, Naaman came to Elisha.

But he was disappointed. Accustomed as Naaman was to discipline and protocol, the prophet Elisha didn't even come out to meet him, and made what appeared to be a silly recommendation: that he bathe in the Jordan River seven times. Naaman knew that the muddy waters of the Jordan were no hygienic match for the crystal-clear mountain spring waters of his native Damascus, and he at first refused. God's requests to all of us seem equally silly at times: to put up with disagreeable relatives, to mortify ourselves, to have patience with people with whom we don't see eye-to-eye.

Eventually Naaman, conforming to the pleas of his servants, performed the suggested ritual baths in the Jordan (v. 14). Thereupon his skin became as clear as that of a little child. And his cure was more than physical: It had reached his whole person. So he immediately acknowledged the God of Israel as the only true God.

Jesus' reference to Elijah, Elisha, and Naaman was a powerful example of how the God of Israel was big enough to be the God of hostile Syria and every other nation. The Jewish monopoly of God's mercy was broken and the curative power of God's compassion was available to one and all. For free! Whenever Catholics, liberal or conservative, think they have a monopoly on truth, holiness, or salvation, this is a good story to remember. The people of Nazareth failed to understand that, with God, love is present wherever human need is found. No one was going to tell *them* that religion had to go so far as Elijah traveling to Sidon or Elisha cleansing a Syrian!

For Israelites, these were fighting words. The people in the synagogue thought Jesus blasphemous in identifying himself with Elijah and Elisha, arrogant in thinking himself better than they, insulting in his mentioning that foreigners would heed a prophet better than they would. Within themselves they asked of Jesus the question often asked of anyone who dares to speak out for God: "Who do you think you are?"

At the beginning of the episode, the eyes of all in the synagogue had looked intently at Jesus (v. 20). By the end of the episode, they looked no farther than their eyes could see, and showed fierce hatred: They led him to the brow of the hill on which their town had been built, intending to toss him over its edge to his death (v. 29). But because his time had not yet come, he walked right through them and went away (v. 30). When in the Father's wisdom the time for the end of Jesus' ministry would arrive, Jesus would be led to another hill, Calvary, outside another city, Jerusalem, there to be put to death for all the human race.

Jesus' sacrifice became possible because of the largeness of divine love. We ought to practice Jesus' kind of love by word and example — in prophetically speaking out God's truth, and in honoring others who do so. Prophecy isn't so much picturing the future as it is challenging people to faithful observance of obligations.

We're reminded of Nathaniel Hawthorne's short story, "The Great Stone Face," in which a small town in New England waited for the coming of a prophet and holy man who would look like the features of a stone outcropping in a local hillside. They waited and waited, but no one ever seemed to come, and the village lost hope and spirit. One day an old man of the town died and, as he was laid out, someone noticed that he looked like the face in the hill. He had been with them all the time and they never recognized him until it was too late!

We're now engaged in the ongoing preparation for Baptism by our catechumens, and our renewal at Easter. All the baptized belong to Christ who died and rose for us. We have the responsibility to profess our faith publicly and to participate in the apostolic and missionary activity of his Church. It's for this that we have the sacraments, the nourishment of the Word of God, and the other spiritual helps of the Church (*Catechism of the Catholic Church*, ##1269-70).

Tuesday, Third Week of Lent
Dn 3:25, 34-43; Mt 18:21-35

Forgiveness

A story is told of a priest in whose parish was a woman who deeply loved God. In fact, the woman claimed that at night she often had visions in which she talked with Jesus and he talked with her. The priest, however, was skeptical of her claim, so to test the visions he said to her, "You say that you actually speak directly with Jesus in your visions? Then let me ask you a favor. The next time you have one of these visions, I want you to ask Jesus what terrible sin your priest committed when he was a young man."

The sin the priest spoke of was something he had done in secret, and no one knew about it except him and the Lord. This years-old sin, however, was such a burden of guilt to him that he was unable to freely experience joy or peace, and was unable to free himself to live in the present. He wanted forgiveness, but felt he never could be forgiven fully.

The woman agreed to ask the priest's question the next time of prayer and went home. When she returned to the church later, the priest said, "Well, did Jesus visit you in your dreams?"

"Yes, he did," replied the woman.

"And did you ask him what sin I committed when I was young?" he asked rather apprehensively.

"Yes, I asked him."

"Well, what did he say?"

She quietly responded, "He said, 'I don't remember.'"

The idea of forgiveness may still be accepted in theory, but in practice with some people it's at a discount. For crimes like pedophilia or genocide, forgiveness has become unthinkable. We may be able to conceive of forgiveness for Judas Iscariot, but to suggest that a repentant Hitler might not be beyond the eventual scope of God's mercy would be considered outlandish. Yet in today's first reading the prayer of the suffering Azariah is a supplication of the community, including a confession of national guilt.

Forgiveness is unique. To forgive isn't the same as to *excuse*, which means to try to remove blame from some fault without further consideration. Nor does to forgive mean to *condone*, which may indicate accepting without protest some reprehensible action because of circumstances — for example, the brutality of the bullfight or institutionalized capital punishment permitted by a culture. It's not the same as *pardon*, either, which may indicate waiving of punishment or censure.

Real guilt — the pain we feel when we deliberately commit sin — is very healthy. How can we say that something so painful can be healthy? A consciousness of guilt is healthy for a number of reasons. First, because true guilt is the direct consequence of a mature and healthy sense of responsibility. Second, because the pain that it causes instills in us a healthy dread of sin — therefore helping to keep us from ugly behavior. Lastly, in real guilt we know that we've done something wrong, something that needs to be undone; that helps a person to live according to societal, moral, and personal norms. Guilt, like shame, functions as an emotion of self-evaluation.

There's a great difference between real guilt and neurotic guilt. Unhealthy neurotic guilt cripples those who live with it as they endlessly hold themselves responsible for negative past events. Even much later, they seem unable to let go of judgmental thoughts, like a rape victim thinking continuously, "I shouldn't have been alone at that time of night." These kinds of thoughts bring on depression, a squashing of legitimate self-esteem, and feelings that one deserves punishment — feelings that sabotage relationships. Unhealthy guilt has an intensity out of proportion to what happened; there's no end in sight.

People in an unhealthy guilt cycle need to ask themselves some questions. Are they punishing themselves for something they did years ago? What do they get out of beating themselves? Is it a matter of pride that they can't accept themselves as they are? When false, neurotic guilt then loses its hold — which takes place only gradually — we can devote more energy toward creatively living in the present and more freely moving into the future.

Authentic guilt springs from genuine wrongdoing and flows from a well-formed conscience. People who have authentic guilt can assess behaviors or omissions honestly. They can acknowledge their wrongdoing, express sorrow, ask for forgiveness from God and others, and try to atone. Then they let the guilt go. Individuals with "good guilt" accept their misdeeds and don't return to them.

To *forgive* true guilt means to give up resentment or claim to requital for an offense. It's to cease to feel resentment against a wrong committed, to give up any claim to requital from or retribution upon an offender.

If we lose forgiveness, we can lose that of which forgiveness is a part: the ability to give and receive love. An unforgiving attitude can have the effect of snow in Antarctica. We often think of Antarctica as a land of perpetual blizzards. Actually, the snowfall there is usually less than two inches a year. The problem is that in the extreme cold the snow doesn't melt. It continues to pile up. There are places in Antarctica where the snow is more than two miles deep and has been there for more than a million years. If we let a feeling of injury build up, it can produce a cold pileup. Forgiveness, on the other hand, melts the resentment and allows love and joy to flourish.

Without forgiveness, we're condemned to live with resentment or guilt. Without forgiveness, instead of human fellowship there will be separate individual prisons — people walled off from one another. Forgiveness frees the forgiver — and the person who accepts forgiveness — to love and to grow.

Forgiveness means *accepting people as they are:* the spouse for being a klutz, the relative for being noisy, the friend for always being late, the stranger for getting in our way. Forgiveness is *taking a risk* — making ourselves vulnerable. Some would call it foolishness, but to renew our commitment even to the friend who has betrayed our trust is to trust *myself* to handle being hurt again. Forgiveness is *accepting an apology* — graciously. Forgiveness is *a way of living:* developing a habit by pardoning others for the little everyday hurts and annoyances — and pardoning ourselves for small things, too.

And forgiveness *isn't conditional*: "I'll forgive you *if* you'll apologize (or change, or make amends)." Forgiveness is *a decision*. That decision is a first step. What happens then depends upon the individual. Forgiveness is *showing mercy* — not only when there's an excuse for what was done, but *even when the injury has been deliberate*. In short, forgiveness is *choosing to love*. Forgiveness is, in fact, the *final* form of love, and *wholehearted* forgiveness is so loving that it's God-like. Nothing speaks of the radical nature of Jesus' message more than his teachings on forgiveness.

It's ironic that in today's gospel it's St. Peter who asked about forgiving another. After the resurrection he would be one of the first to need the Lord's forgiveness. But right now he understood that if God forgives, as Jesus taught and showed, then God's disciple must be ready to forgive, too. So Peter wanted to know *how often* he should forgive (v. 21). He suggested seven times, meaning by that number *perfection*, completeness — as in seven days for the creation of the world. He thought he was being generous and expected warm commendation for it. Jesus' answer, that we should forgive seventy times seven times (v. 22), is also symbolic, meaning without limit: all the time. Forgiveness is a matter of love, not of how many times.

Then Jesus likened the kingdom of heaven to a king (v. 23), in a parable whose details shouldn't be allegorized. The conduct of the king, an Oriental despot, isn't a model for the mercy of God. The significant item is the comparative amounts owed to and by the king's high official: millions versus practically nothing (v. 28).

The king of that time had the power to order his official to be sold, along with his wife, his children, and all his property in payment of the debt (v. 25), because a man's wife and children were regarded as his property. To take a man's family in lieu of his debt was common practice, especially among the pagans; among the Hebrews the Mosaic Law tried to mitigate its evils. The guilty official threw himself on the mercy of the king.

Despite the servant's pleas for mercy (v. 29), the official put him in a debtor's prison (v. 30) until his relatives and friends would get the money. Before we condemn the official, let's remember the times when we've self-centeredly elbowed our way through life by being hard, cold, and unforgiving. The master, hearing of his official's hardness (v. 31), sent for him (v. 32) and addressed to him the point of the parable: Shouldn't you have had pity, as I had pity on you? (v. 33). The lesson is that the magnitude of God's forgiveness makes it ridiculous for us not to forgive one another our petty offenses.

Another part of the story that grates harshly on our ears is that the master handed him over to the torturers (v. 34). Tyrants, especially in the Orient, made use of torture in order to wring from their victims the confession of a hidden source of wealth or to have the victim's loved ones pay the required money. (The world's despots still use torture to wring confessions.) In this case the debt was so large that it couldn't be paid back. Jesus' conclusion is that his heavenly Father will do the same to all who won't forgive their brother or sister — from their heart (v. 35).

What should our forgiveness be like? It's a fearful thought that others may only see God as they see Him in us! Our forgiveness should be like our heavenly Father's: total and joyous. To begin, we should acknowledge our feeling of resentment at an injury that's been done. Take some action as soon as possible: a letter, a word, a kindness, a hug, an apology, a prayer. Our action may be the key that will free us from guilt and bring peace. If the other doesn't want our forgiveness, we give it silently, in our heart. For our own transgressions, if we can't say "I'm sorry," we pray for the strength to say it.

If God forgives so easily, why bother examining our consciences, or praying about our offenses, or going to the sacrament of Reconciliation? Why not just live life, do what we will, rely upon God's love, and let the devil take the hindmost? Well, if we did that, we'd lose all sense of sin, lose a sense of where we are in our spiritual life. Our sensitivity would become coarse and our behavior crude, we'd lose our appreciation of the breadth and depth of God's love for us, and we'd have no ideal upon which to model our lives.

Yet forgiveness can be a difficult business. It's often easy for us to love the whole world, but hard to forgive the person who lives or works next to us. But what's impossible to nature is possible to grace. It was hard for Peter; it's hard for us.

Forgiveness is humankind's deepest need and at the same time our highest achievement. Let's contribute to the healing forgiveness that we and our world so greatly crave.

Dt 4:1, 5-9; Mt 5:17-19

Continuing Our Search for Holiness

As we come to the midpoint of Lent, it's legitimate to ask ourselves, "How'm I doing?" If our Lenten focus has been on "less"
— less food, less entertainment, less wasting time — it was a good
beginning. Now as we head down the homestretch of the Road
to Resurrection, today's readings offer a clear clue for concen-
trating on fulfillment in a positive way.

The Torah for the Jews — the Law of Moses — was the most
complete and precise expression of God's will they had. In the
Torah, God put into words the vision of what the people of Israel should be. For them, it was the summary of all wisdom,
human and divine: the self-revelation of God, a complete and
secure guide of conduct. Jesus grew to adulthood as a devout Jew
living by that Law.

The Book of Deuteronomy, a section of which we read in
today's first reading, is a part of the Torah. A law book, Deuteronomy presents a vision of the Mosaic Law as part of the relationship of faithfulness between God and His people. This fifth book
of the Bible was among Jesus' favorites for several reasons, among
them Deuteronomy's sense of compassion and devotion. It spoke
to his best self more easily than many other books of the Bible.
Jesus spontaneously turned to this book: in his temptation ordeal
(Mt 4:1-11), for example, and in answering the questions about
the first and greatest commandment (Mk 12:28-34).

In today's gospel, Jesus emphasized that he didn't come to
abolish the Mosaic Law, but to fulfill it. Using the word "fulfill"
about fifteen times in Matthew's gospel, Jesus wants to emphasize that his purpose is to complete, perfect, round out, top off,
and bring to maturity the principles and practices of the Old
Testament.

His emphasis is on mercy, not legalistic minutiae; on far-reaching love, not destructive petty details; and on positive heart-felt commitment, not external prohibitions. Jesus had come to give the Old Law all the richness that the Jews believed it had. Because Jesus saw the current leaders as blind guides, he repeatedly rejected their *misinterpretations* of the Law and their burdensome regulations. At the same time, Jesus' law isn't entirely new, but rather the natural development and perfection of the Old Law.

It's difficult for us to realize how shocking Jesus' teaching was to the Jews of his day. He was pointing out some inadequacies in what the leaders of the people considered to be the most sacred and wisest writings in the world. Prior to their entry into the Promised Land, as today's first reading shows, Moses reminded the people of the centrality of the Law. In their faithfulness to this Law, God's people could become a source of light and hope to all other nations who might look on their fidelity to their relationships, contracts, and customs. The Rabbis had standard phrases for commenting on the Law, like, "Thus says the Lord"; the implication was that no one could argue with that. Yet Jesus put forward his own teaching; he spoke with an authority that held the crowds spellbound. No one had dared do this before.

The Gospel of Jesus Christ is the way of eternal insight. When reflected on in prayer, God in Jesus can answer our ultimate questions about life and meaning. The laws of Christ and his Church in the modern world are to be a source of joy and praise to God. They're also to distinguish the Christian in the world. The ancient cry, "See these Christians, how they love one another," was a recognition that no other people had a commandment to match the Christian rule of love.

Lent is a time of spiritual purification, so that God's least wish becomes an absolute command for us. The Lord calls us to more than legal compliance, however. He invites us to spiritual perfection. If we're to arrive at holiness, we must each day practice many human and supernatural virtues: faith, hope, charity, justice, fortitude, industriousness, loyalty, optimism. While acquiring a habit of exercising each virtue, we must at the same time be sincere, truthful, balanced, calm, and patient.

We'll be wounded many times in our life. We'll make mistakes. Some people will call them failures. But failure is really God's way of saying, "Excuse me, you're moving in the wrong direction." We become ever more aware that the Christian life demands purification from past sins, an increase in virtue, and rising from failures to correspond with grace.

Especially during Lent the Church invites us to grow in virtue — that is, in habits of doing good. Through cultivating *human* virtues as well as the divine — resilience, loyalty, truthfulness, affection, courtesy — we prepare ourselves in the best possible way for the action of the Holy Spirit.

Thursday, Third Week of Lent
Jr 7:23-28; Lk 11:14-23

Listen

In today's excerpt from Jeremiah the prophet, the Lord's complaint with the Hebrews is that they didn't *listen* to Him, and therefore didn't obey. It's a complaint that may at times be made of us. True listening — to God or one another — doesn't mean simply maintaining a polite silence.

There are at least four ways in which we can *fail to listen* adequately and thus cause serious damage: refusing to listen; pretending to listen; listening without patience; and listening without an adequate response. There are many *unworthy* reasons why people listen in general: to a spouse to keep peace, to children out of frustration, to an employer because there's no other way out. There are "listenings" of criticism, of resentment, of superiority, of indifference.

True listening means trying to see the matter at hand the way the speaker sees it. This means not merely passive sympathy, which is feeling for the other, but active empathy, which is going out to the other. Just as respect is the first step on the road to justice, empathy is the first step on the road to love. Many of our young don't want to take that step — or even the prior step of noticing others outside their tested-and-trusted cliques. If that's true, then any parent or teacher who chatters away idly to them about the selflessness and altruism of Christianity might as well shout in Mandarin to the deaf. Empathy helps to develop the very humanizing virtue of forgiveness.

Television and films have the effect of encouraging people to zip up their Teflon cocoon and let the rest of the world roll by. A great many of the (literally) blockbuster movies bristle with explosions and mayhem until those scenes are no more able to move — or shock — than the explosions in a video game. We're also besieged with public service announcements showing children with great glistening, mournful eyes, flies drinking their tears, making us feel helplessly soul-bruised, to the point where it just becomes too much. We flick the dial, turn the page, render ourselves amnesiacs about it. It's just too much overload for anyone to watch, listen to, or read about.

One psychiatrist said that if you can't feel pain — your own or another's — you're not going to be able to feel anything else either. True listening requires entering imaginatively into the other's situation and trying to understand a frame of reference different from our own. There are four crucial steps to good listening: stepping out of my own world; entering into your world; sensing your deepest feelings; and giving an adequate response.

Sensitive listening comes across as very special praise. It makes the other person feel affirmed and worthwhile.

When we've given all our attention, as though the other person were the only one in the world at that moment — and that's what good listening communicates — we touch the other deeply. We've taken the trouble to enter into their world and to see things from their point of view. They feel understood, cared for, accepted.

Careful listening touches a person more deeply than any word of praise that we could possibly say. Words are, in fact, easy to say. They don't require the self-giving that good listening demands. Words can be suspect as possible flattery. Our praise in listening is more indirect, but perhaps less suspect than mere words of support. The only way we can truly listen to God and other people is through sensitivity. And then, as we said in today's Responsorial Psalm (95): "Today, if you hear His voice, harden not your heart."

An important requirement for hearing is to get rid of preconceived ideas. In Jesus' life, despite the fact that God was speaking to the Jews in ways that they should have understood, they wanted God's signs to be accommodated to *them.* But God is in His own image, not in ours, and Jesus was showing Him as He is.

Listening to the voice of God will result in a life chock full of meaning. This may involve a turning around of one's whole value system — away from self and toward intense service in behalf of God and others. Supereminently as a result of listening, we will recognize such values as our call to holiness, the definition of true greatness, the meaning of faith and trust, and a good perspective on joy and suffering. Even the Chinese fortune cookie says, "From listening comes wisdom and from speaking regret."

Our listening is not to result in mere understanding or fine words: We're to *act* upon what we hear. Having listened to God's voice and truly heard, we "let go, and let God." What symphony

conductor Herbert Von Karajan said about conducting applies
to life: "Technique you can learn. But what comes out of it is what
you give as a human being." To listen to Jesus' message is to give
oneself to constantly renewing one's cooperation with God's
grace; those who only take and never give find it hard to justify
their existence.

Many people — all of us at one time or other — confess
God with our lips and deny Him with our lives. It's seldom hard
to recite our Creed, but it's often hard to live the Christian life.
If we don't pay attention to this difficult job of listening, we can
become like the people in today's gospel. Because they didn't listen in good faith, they became guilty of a great sin: calumny. They
couldn't deny the reality of Jesus' cures, so they claimed that he
was possessed — worse, possessed by Beelzebul, a detested demon. The first part of Beelzebul's name is akin to "Baal," which
can mean "Lord." The second part can mean "of the Flies," or
may refer to excrement. In neither case is the name flattering.
Further, they attributed to Jesus a sort of black magic, whereby
he was expelling little demons by the great demon.

The calumny of these people was inspired by a cold venom.
But although truth, like a house built on a firm foundation, has
endurance, a lie, like a bullet, has speed. And their non-listen-
ing calumny was of a kind to turn even people of good will from
Jesus. Jesus' answering argument made eminent sense: the power
of evil would certainly not allow itself to be divided, because that
would ensure its defeat. Put another way, said Jesus, anyone
wanting to plunder another's house must first put the owner
under restraint.

The parable of the strong man able to guard his house until a stronger appears is appropriate for Lent. As long as we're in
control of ourselves, the power of evil is weak. Our strength
against evil derives from renewed hearts and minds that a spe-
cially graced season like Lent provides.

Lent is a good time for developing and improving a quiet

listening to the voice of God. Listening, as referred to in the prophet Jeremiah, is a prerequisite for having a faith relationship with God. There's a need for practice and growth in our ability to pay close attention to God. And let's listen seriously to our Church when she teaches with authority. The Church is called to continue teaching with Jesus' authority. It's a demanding task.

During the rest of this Lent, let's begin to add a little more quiet receptivity to prayer, gradually working toward a balance between listening and speaking.

Friday, Third Week of Lent

Ho 14:2-10; Mk 12:28-34

Unrestrained Love

In the eighth century before Christ, when the Jews were split into two nations, Israel in the north and Judea in the south, Hosea was a prophet to the stylish northern kingdom, Israel. Its people had been taken over by the Assyrians and deported. Today's reading from Hosea looks past the Assyrian takeover to a future time when the people would return to God with minds and hearts renewed, reminiscent of the spirit of Lent and of today's gospel.

But from the time of Hosea to that of Jesus the Jews who wanted to worship God correctly had a problem. They had always to keep in mind the 613 written legal prescriptions and many more oral ones of the Law of Moses. In today's gospel, a scribe came up and asked Jesus an honest question that people ask often: Which is the *first* of all the commandments? (v. 28). Jesus' answer gave two texts from the Jewish Scriptures; they would come to underlie all of New Testament morality as well as they had of the Old.

The first part of Jesus' answer was from the Book of Deuteronomy (6:4). It's part of Moses' poignant farewell address as he was about to die, just before his people entered the Promised Land. The words are the keynote of Deuteronomy: the great Jewish prayer, called from its opening word the *Shema*, which means in our modern vernacular, "Listen up!"

The *Shema* would become many things to Israel. It was the Jewish morning and evening prayer. It would be "words to die by" as well as "words to live by." It became the first sentence every Jewish child commits to memory, the prayer which all religious Jews hope to have on their lips when they die. Hebrew martyrs went to their death with these words on their lips. The words would be written on tiny scrolls and put into the prayer-boxes (phylacteries) that adorn foreheads and wrists while at prayer. The words would be wrapped in the *mezuzah*, the little container which is to this day affixed to the entrances of the homes of devout Jews to remind them of the word of God as they come and go.

The prayer begins with the basic principle of the entire Mosaic Law: The Lord alone is God. As our God is unique, so the basic human response to God must also be unique and undivided: "You shall love the Lord your God with all your heart, with all your soul, with all your mind, and with all your strength" (v. 30). The people of the time considered the heart the center of both knowing and feeling, the soul the principle of life and the source of all one's energies, and the mind the center of perception. The text means we're to love God with everything we have: a love which is dynamic, not phlegmatic; outgoing, not introverted; performed with commitment, not lackadaisical.

Jesus added another part: "You shall love your neighbor as yourself" (v. 31) — words from the Book of Leviticus (19:18). This second precept is the manifestation of the first. Love of God issues forth in proper love of ourselves and other people. Many personably warm people who don't believe in God love other people, but it's really only when we love others *in God* that human beings become *deeply* lovable — not with sentimentality, but with commitment. There's an intimate connection between our love of God and love of our neighbor.

One aspect of love of neighbor is hospitality. In biblical times, hospitality was considered an important virtue. God appears to all of us in various guises — a child needing an education, a neighbor in pain, a cause that deserves our support — and we show hospitality to God by responding. This is the height of being alive.

If both love of God and love of neighbor are in the Jewish Scriptures, what's new about Jesus' answer? To begin, the Jews divided their precepts into "heavy" and "light," and rabbinical tradition classified Jesus' second precept as "lighter" than the first. Jesus gave both precepts *equal weight. This* was new, and has no parallel in all Jewish literature. Another facet of newness was that Jesus gave a completely new interpretation of "neighbor." For him, the word has the widest meaning possible. It includes every member of the human race. He would die for everyone. In Christian charity, people and God aren't merely side by side; they're inseparably one. We can't honor another person without blessing God, nor adore God without loving all human beings. We're all God's creatures (*Catechism of the Catholic Church,* #2069). Lent is a time for practicing deep love of God and a time to reach out to our neighbor.

Love of God and neighbor must begin with proper love of self. Whereas in the theological order of priority God and neighbor come first, in the psychological order we begin with proper love of self. Unless we have sufficient and proper self-love, we can go no further. Without *being* loved it's impossible to love. The experience of love is not only what makes the world go 'round: It's what makes the ride worthwhile. Lent is a good time to examine whether our love of God is adequate, our love of others is sufficient, and our love of "self" is correct. The best example of abiding by these laws is Jesus. For us, Lent is a time for *metanoia*, of converting to the Lord who has loved us with an eternal love. Jesus is everything.

That Jesus is everything is well illustrated by a story of a wealthy man and his son who loved to collect rare works of art. They had everything in their collection, from Picasso to Raphael. They would often sit together and admire their great works of art.

When the Vietnam conflict broke out, the son went to war. He was very courageous and died in battle while rescuing another soldier. The father was notified and grieved deeply for his only son.

About a month later, just before Christmas, there was a knock at the door. A young man stood at the door with a large package in his hands.

He said, "Sir, you don't know me, but I'm a soldier for whom your son gave his life. He saved many lives that day, and he was carrying me to safety when a bullet struck him in the heart; he died instantly. He often talked about you, and your love for art."

The young man held out his package. "I know this isn't much. I'm not really a great artist, but I think your son would have wanted you to have this."

The father opened the package. It was a portrait of his son, painted by the young man. The father stared in awe at the way the soldier had captured the personality of his son in the painting. The father was so drawn to his son's eyes that his own eyes welled up with tears. He thanked the young man and offered to pay him for the picture.

"Oh no, sir, I could never repay what your son did for me. It's a gift."

The father hung the portrait over his mantle. Every time visitors came to his home he took them to see the portrait of his son before he showed them any of the great paintings he had collected.

A few months later the man died. There was a great auction of his paintings. Many wealthy people gathered, excited over seeing the great paintings and having an opportunity to purchase one. On the platform sat the painting of the son.

The auctioneer pounded his gavel. "We will start the bidding with this picture of the son. Who will bid for it?" There was silence. Then a voice in the back of the room shouted, "We want to see the famous paintings. Skip this one."

But the auctioneer persisted. "Will someone bid for this painting? Who will start the bidding? $100, $200?"

Another voice shouted angrily. "We didn't come to see this painting. We came to see the van Goghs, the Rembrandts. Get on with the real bids!"

But still the auctioneer continued. "The son! The son! Who'll take the son?"

Finally a voice came from the back of the room. It was the longtime gardener of the man and his son. "I'll give $10 for the painting." Being a poor man, it was all he could afford.

"We have $10, who will bid $20?"

"Give it to him for $10. Let's see the masters."

"$10 is the bid. Won't someone bid $20?"

The crowd was becoming impatient. They didn't want the picture of the son. They wanted the more worthy investments for their collections. The auctioneer pounded the gavel. "Going once, twice, SOLD for $10!"

A man sitting in the second row shouted, "Now let's get on with the auction!"

The auctioneer laid down his gavel. "I regret to say, the auction is over."

"What about the paintings?"

"I'm sorry. When I was called to conduct this auction, I was told of a secret stipulation in the will. I wasn't allowed to reveal

that stipulation until now. Only the painting of the son would
be auctioned. Whoever bought that would inherit the entire estate, including the paintings. The man who took the son gets everything!"

God gave his Son 2,000 years ago to die on the cross. Much
like the auctioneer, God's message today is, "The man who takes
the Son gets everything!"

Saturday, Third Week of Lent
Ho 6:1-6; Lk 18:9-14

Humility in Approaching God

Sociological studies show many things about prayer, among them
the following. This week more of us will pray than will go to
work, or exercise, or have sexual relations. Also, many spouses
readily discuss their sex lives, but have to struggle to talk about
prayer. And serious prayer usually begins after the age of about
thirty, when the illusion that we're masters of our own fate fades
and we develop a deeper need to call on the Master of the Universe. The studies show, further, that even on talk shows that
deal with controversial topics, prayer is never mentioned.

In today's gospel Jesus talks about prayer in the story of the
Pharisee and the tax collector (v. 9). These two went up to what
was in Luke's gospel a very privileged place, the Temple, to pray
(v. 10). Or, as the humorist put it, "Two men went up to the
Temple to pray; one did, and the other didn't!"

The Pharisee was a good man. He came from the *parisim*,
meaning a group separate, set apart. They tried to live up to the
sacred Law of Moses completely. You would like the Pharisee as

your next-door neighbor. You could count on him to be honest, to respect your property, and to do everything right. Yet the people gave some of them unflattering nicknames: "Blood-headed Pharisees," for example, because in their attempts to avoid looking at women in the street they bumped into walls; "Bookkeeper Pharisees" for those who kept an exact record of their good deeds to offset their bad ones; and "Wait-A-Minute Pharisees" for those who told people wanting to speak with them to "wait a minute" while they went to perform a good deed. But the true Pharisees were called "Pharisees of Love."

In today's story, the righteousness of the Pharisee considerably exceeded the standards prescribed by the Mosaic Law. For instance, the Law prescribed one day of fast a year (the Day of Atonement), but he, like many Pharisees, held a complete fast, with no food or drink until after sundown, twice a week: Mondays and Thursdays. The Law commanded tithes of farm produce profits; this Pharisee tithed himself on everything.

The Pharisee of Jesus' story was a snob who attributed all his many virtues to his own merits, reminded God of all the good he was doing, and made God out to be in debt to him. He was full of himself; the key word in his prayer was "I." And he used his prayer to speak ill of his fellow human beings. To look down on everyone else when we're doing good, as the Pharisee did, is easy. Our society gives ample opportunity to look down: on people guilty of abortion, for instance, and on homosexuals, indulgers in sex outside marriage, street beggars, drug users, AIDS victims, drunkards. Difficult though it may be to admit, there's something of the Pharisee in each of us.

The ancient Pharisee was perhaps not unlike the modern Joe B. He drives a Jaguar. His son went to Harvard. He has hobnobbed with five Nobel laureates. He's been to football games in $400 front-row seats, exchanged greetings with prominent movie stars, and had the United States Senator from his state to his apartment for dinner. He's on friendly terms with lawyers to the famous and receives an occasional note from his congressman. Like the Pharisee, Mr. B. is also, by his own admission, a snob.

Snobbery is a peculiarly modern disease: a by-product of democracy. The social fluidity that democracy makes possible, allowing people to climb from the bottom to the top of the ladder of social class in a generation or two, provides the breeding ground for snobbery and gives room to exercise condescension, haughtiness, affectation, false deference, and other egregious behavior congenial to the snob.

In the past, your place in the rigid social order was fixed at birth. This explains why Shakespeare, Dante, Aristophanes, and the Bible are basically snob-free. By 1848, however, a large and prosperous commercial class was wreaking havoc on England's old caste system. In that year, when William Makepeace Thackeray wrote his *Book of Snobs* — the first major literary use of the term — they seemed to be everywhere: royal snobs, city snobs, country snobs, military snobs, literary snobs, club snobs, and "dining-out" snobs.

Thackeray claimed that no place proved a more ideal incubator of snobbery than the United States. Living in a country with few built-in class distinctions, people in the United States turned to snobbery as compensation, a means of clarifying what the Constitution failed to: just who was better than whom. Nor did it hurt that the United States was predominantly middle class. To be middle class places one nicely to be both an upward- and a downward-looking snob, simultaneously full of aspiration to rise to the position of those above and of disdain for those below.

The other person in Jesus' story was a tax collector. Tax-collectors of Jesus' time were a group of social outcasts who were considered robbers for Rome. But the very body language of the tax collector of Jesus' story — keeping his distance, raising his eyes to heaven, beating his breast — showed his attitude in prayer. He used for his prayer the opening verse of the Psalm composed by King David to ask God's mercy after his adultery with Bathsheba — a prayer so simple and yet so perfect: "God, be merciful to me, a sinner." Both David and the tax collector knew themselves.

It's as difficult to know ourselves, and often as painful, as it is to peel an onion, which makes us cry. Oscar Wilde once said that "only the shallow know themselves." Examination of the world without is never as personally painful as examination of the world within; because of the pain involved in a life of genuine self-examination, many people steer clear of it. Yet to those dedicated to truth this pain seems relatively unimportant — and less and less important (and therefore less and less painful) the farther you proceed on the path of self-examination.

From childhood on, we acquire superficial identities which, like an onion, layer us as we become what our parents, teachers, and friends want us to be. Desperate for love and approval, we can easily respond to other people by saying, "Yes, I'll bury who I really am and become who you want me to be." But the real us doesn't go away: It lives in the center of our soul and pounds to get out. Then grace, often in the form of a crisis, moves us to start peeling the onion, and maybe crying. When we strip away our false identities, we're left naked until we search for, discover, and treasure our real selves: God's idea of what He wanted us to be when He brought us into being in the first place.

At the end of an art exhibit some time ago, an artist computerized various ways in which we can see ourselves. In an "Age Machine," you could sit back and see how you might look in 25 years. The artist teamed up with some computer programmers to make an aging program, which would stretch and warp digital portraits. She aged the faces of some movie stars. She also reversed the aging process to produce fake baby pictures of other stars.

In another invention, the "Human Race Machine," you could scan your face, and then the computer program altered it to look African, Asian, Indian, Hispanic, or whatever. In still

another invention, the "Anomaly Machine," you could see what
you might look like with various facial deformities. The artist
suggested that nothing is fixed about the human face — not
beauty, youth, race, power, sex, family, species, or godliness.

The artist helped the F.B.I. search for missing children by
envisioning what they would look like years after they had disappeared. This kind of visualization process actually brought
home four children in its first year.

In today's first reading, Hosea speaks of God in terms of in-
discriminate abundance: God will come to us like spring rain that
waters the earth (v. 3). He reminds us that God's true identity is
reliable, life-giving, cleansing, purifying. Like spring rain, God
is the sweet essence of all that lives and grows. Whenever we're
in need, in fear, in despair, or in pain, God will come to us like
the rain — smooth, gentle, and steady. It's the nature of spring
rain to renew and refresh. So it is with God.

The teaching of Jesus about prayer stresses the need to approach God in a humble spirit. We do not speak in an attitude
of Pharisaic pride. "Only when we humbly acknowledge that 'we
do not know how to pray as we ought' are we ready to receive
freely the gift of prayer. 'Man is a beggar before God'" (*Catechism
of the Catholic Church*, #2559).

God tells us through the prophet Hosea that it's love He desires above all else. The end of Jesus' story startled his audience
by having the Pharisee the villain of the piece and the tax collector the hero (v. 14). The tax collector's self-knowledge and humility brought him home in a right relationship with God. Which
of the two are we?

Is 65:17-21; Jn 4:43-54

Embrace Your Renewal

How fast are you going when you seem to be standing still? To someone standing next to you at the equator, zero degrees latitude, you'd appear stationary. To a Martian hovering over the Earth, you'd appear to be spinning at 1,041 miles per hour. From the sun, it would look like you were riding a terrestrial Tilt-A-Whirl and orbiting the home star, the sun, at 60,000 miles per hour. From the edge of the Andromeda Galaxy, Earth would be seen spinning, orbiting, and finally spiraling through the Milky Way at an average of 530,000 miles per hour. Add all this up, and you're traveling at a top speed of 591,041 miles per hour. But the universe is expanding, so it's impossible to know how fast we're really going. Tell all that to the next cop who stops you for speeding!

In still other wonders, by combining observations made using the mighty Keck Telescope in Hawaii and the Hubble Space Telescope, astronomers years ago (1997) discovered the most distant object ever seen, some 13 billion light-years from the earth (the most distant and ancient then discovered). Analysis of the faint light reaching earth from this object has yielded strong hints of how galaxies came into being soon after most scientists say the Big Bang created the universe.

Astronomers now see that object — an infant galaxy — as it was 13 billion years ago, when the universe was only 7 percent of its present age. It takes that long for the light to reach Earth. Although the galaxy is only a quarter the size of our own Milky Way, it's 10 times as bright, studded with dazzling clumps of new stars. It's illuminated by supernova explosions going off like a string of firecrackers. The galaxy contains many very small but intensely bright knots, each apparently a region where many stars are forming.

Those thoughts give us a small inkling into God's physical creation. In today's first reading, God promises through Isaiah to create new heavens and a new earth. It's a prophetic picture in highly imaginative form of the joys that will belong to the people of Jerusalem when they come home from the Exile. We, too, long for the Holy City of God's Kingdom. What do we hope for? That we will see our loved ones again; that we will be re-united with a wife or husband; that we will see our children who died too young; that we will be free from pain and illness. All of that is within the power of God.

According to the gospel of St. John, Jesus' public ministry can be summarized in connection with a number of Jesus' deeds which are able to be interpreted as having spiritual significance — hence John's not calling them miracles, but "signs." It's not the miraculous element that he regards as having the greatest significance, but rather the spiritual meaning. They're "signs" of the power of God which brings about a transformation in people's lives.

John's use of the miracle stories is different from that of the Synoptics: Sts. Matthew, Mark, and Luke. In the Synoptics, the purpose of the miracles appears to be to present evidence to support the claim that Jesus was the true Messiah. In their case, the historical accuracy of the event would be crucial. In John, only seven miracles are reported and in none of them is the real meaning of the story dependent on historical accuracy. Not that John has any doubts about their historical accuracy; he just doesn't discuss the point. He has something else in mind that he considers far more important: the spiritual lessons to be derived.

The fact that there are seven signs-miracles in John's gospel is important. In the Jewish view, the number seven means perfection or completion. The seven signs and their meanings are: (1) turning water into wine (2:1-12): Jesus is the source of life; (2) healing a nobleman's son (4:46-54), the "sign" in today's gospel: Jesus is master over distance; (3) healing a lame man at the pool of Bethesda (5:1-17): Jesus is master over time; (4) feeding more than 5,000 people (6:1-14): Jesus is the bread of life; (5) walking on water and stilling a storm (6:15-21): Jesus is master over nature; (6) healing a man blind from birth (9:1-41): Jesus is the light of the world; (7) raising Lazarus from the dead (11:17-45): Jesus has power over death.

As we enter this fourth week of Lent we know that it won't be long before the rejoicing and happiness of the Easter season will be with us. In today's poignant gospel story, Jesus gives us a sneak preview of Easter. In it, he assures a concerned father, whose child was near death, that his son would live. Now it won't be long before God's own Son will be near death; our trust in Jesus' word assures us that he will live, now and forever.

As Jesus had said elsewhere (Mt 13:57; Mk 6;4; Lk 4:24), no one esteems a prophet in his own country (v. 44). Jesus had said essentially the same thing to the Galileans in the synagogue at Nazareth when because of their unbelief he couldn't work many miracles there. Here in John, "his own country" meant his people in Judea; in the Synoptics, "his own country" meant Galilee.

The royal official approaching Jesus was a Jew, probably in the service of Herod Antipas. Jesus was in Cana, and the official's son was sick at Capernaum, about 16 miles away. The official's faith wasn't perfect: He begged Jesus to come down (v. 47), not thinking that Jesus could work a miracle from a distance. Jesus' initial retort — that unless you people see signs and wonders you won't believe (v. 48) — was aimed at the Jews as a class.

Jesus' direction that the official go on his way, because his son lives (v. 50) put the man's faith to the test of accepting Jesus' word without proof. The hope expressed in Jesus' words is the desire of all who are coming from sin to forgiveness, from death to new life in the sacraments of Baptism and Reconciliation and

at Easter. Trusting the words of Jesus seems so natural in this
story. We rarely find it so clear and simple! Usually, we're either
very unsure about what to do or we discount what might happen. We want certainty! Yet the direction for our lives is usually
not that precise or apparent. We need to trust that God is with
us. We're often not sure what we "hear" at first, so we need to
ponder it a while. We also have to trust our prayer, our intuition,
and the promises in Scripture which assure us of God's guidance.

The official arrived home only the next day. Since he believed, he could hardly show great haste to verify his son's cure;
besides, rest for his animals and followers was needed. On the way,
he learned that his son had been cured at about the same time that
Jesus had assured him of the cure (v. 51). His faith lost all reserve,
and he and his whole household became believers (v. 53).

Tuesday, Fourth Week of Lent
Ezk 47:1-9, 12; Jn 5:1-3, 5-16

Persistence in Faith

The facts of the cure of the man in today's gospel are in the story.
The "Sheep Pool" was near the "Sheep Gate," so-called because
originally that was the way the sacrificial lambs were brought to
the Temple. Herod the Great had had the pool constructed into
quite an elaborate structure. Even today, its ruins show the
magnificence of his plans.

It's hard to understand that someone could be cured by being the first to enter the water after some sort of stirrings, but
this was the popular belief. Among the blind, lame, and paralyzed who sought cures there was a man who had been crippled

for thirty-eight years — since before Jesus was born. If he'd been coming to the pool every day for the thirty-eight years, that would have been 13,870 times.

For all that time there was no one to give the sick man a helping hand to reach the healing waters. Contrasting with that coldness was the compassion of Jesus. The man's persistence was admirable. In old age, Pierre Renoir, the great French painter, suffered from arthritis. Even though it was so bad that it twisted and cramped his hands, Renoir, grasping a brush with only his fingertips, continued to paint. Each movement caused him such stabbing pain that one day his artist friend, Henri Matisse, asked why he persisted in painting at the expense of such torture. Renoir replied, "The pain passes, but the beauty remains."

Jesus cured the man and told him to pick up his mat and walk. Among the 39 classes of work forbidden by their Mosaic Law on the Sabbath was carrying an article from one place to another. The guilt was to be fixed on the instigator of the act, and the penalty was severe. Officialdom would leave a human being to suffer while they upheld laws that were intended to help people. Jesus' attitude, which he had expressed elsewhere (Mk 2:27), is that the Sabbath was made for people, not people for the Sabbath.

After the cured man had been interrogated by the Jewish officials, Jesus found him in the Temple; evidently the man had gone there to give thanks. One of the greatest Russian poets (Tyutchev) once said that gratitude is the purest form of love. It may not be the highest form of love, but it's the purest. Why? Because when you're full of gratitude there isn't room for anything like recrimination, or desire for revenge, or any other hostile thoughts or acts.

The cured man didn't seem to know much of what had gone on, other than that he'd been cured. Jesus admonished him to avoid his sins. That was the end of the miracle but, as always with the gospel of St. John, this sign was a great deal more than a cure.

For one thing, there was the symbolism of water. As with today's first reading from Ezekiel, water symbolizes great blessings — life for people and for all living things. Water has the double effect of destroying and delivering. To the people living along a river that rampages in a flood through towns and farmlands, water presents nightmares of devastation. To people living in drought-plagued areas, water is a refreshing phenomenon.

At the very dawn of creation God's Holy Spirit breathed on the waters, making them the wellspring of holiness. The deluge in the Book of Genesis (Chapters 6-9) destroyed the wicked but delivered Noah and his family. The Red Sea in the Book of Exodus (Chapter 14) delivered God's people by destroying their pursuing persecutors. In the waters of the Jordan Jesus was baptized. Water and blood flowed from Jesus' side as he hung upon the cross. After his Resurrection Jesus told his disciples to go out and baptize all nations. At Baptism we're reminded that God has made water a rich symbol of the grace He gives us. Our current season being Lent, the Church also holds out great expectations for the catechumens soon to receive the water of Baptism with its abundance of blessings.

After this incident Jesus delivered a long discourse in which he explained that this man's healing was only a symbol of the kind of life Jesus gives — not just biological life, but a spiritual energy that binds all the different levels of our life together. Jesus had already instructed his followers (Jn 3:31-36) that the Son's mission from the Father is to "give life" to those who believe; he repeats that idea here.

What is this "life" that Jesus gives? Some people whose physical lives have been deformed from birth have sued doctors and states for the "right not to be born." One mother of a girl born with club feet, no thumbs, and other serious physical and mental disabilities said that if she had known about these problems she would have aborted the child. She sued for wrongful life. One doctor lost a case with a woman whose child was born with Down's Syndrome, because he had failed to get pre-natal tests. Medical associations explain that the aim of medical treatment is to heal, alleviate, or prevent illnesses and disabilities, not to kill the sick and disabled.

There are public policy considerations against the recognition of such claims. They include the precious nature of human life and the erosive effect that the acceptance of such claims have upon the value to be accorded to human life. There is also the impact that the recognition of this class of claims would have upon the self-esteem of those born with disabilities and upon their perceived worthiness by other members of society. If wrongful life claims were recognized, mothers could be open to being sued for continuing with a pregnancy whose birth might be considered a burden to society.

Beginning with the last verse of today's gospel, in which the real issue is Jesus' claim to equality with God, John's gospel indicates that Jesus was now stepping onto the public stage in confrontation with the officialdom of Judaism. Everywhere he turns there will be some form of hostility against him.

There are many avenues here for Lenten reflections. For one thing, from all the gospel accounts of Jesus curing the sick, we know that he looked for faith in those to be healed — that simple, child-like openness to grace — and for persistence. We ought to persist faithfully in our daily spiritual disciplines even when they don't appear to be having any dramatic results. And little by little let's develop a self-sacrificing willingness to risk being rejected, as the man in today's gospel did, and as Jesus himself had, in order to stand up publicly for what's right.

Today, we're looking forward to the completion of the Rite of Christian Initiation and the baptism of candidates as well as the renewal of our baptismal vows at the Easter Vigil; once again, we're reminded that it's the word of Jesus that gives the sacrament of Baptism its saving power. When his word and water come together, sin is destroyed and we're delivered unto eternal life.

Power and Tenderness

Both of today's Scripture readings contain notions of God's power and, at the same time, His tenderness.

The Book of Isaiah was written as Judah's Exile in Babylon was about to end. During that Exile, many questions arose. For example, the people asked why this tragedy had struck them. They acknowledged that they had committed some wrongs, but in comparison with surrounding pagan cultures they considered themselves devout. It seemed that God had abandoned them.

Isaiah told them that God had not left them, and offered a vision of restoration. God will answer prayers, said Isaiah, at a time which He knows best. The exiles in Babylon may think that their prayers weren't being heard, but God was delaying His marvelous blessings to a favorable time. To assure them that God never abandons people, Isaiah gave one of the most touching images in the Bible. Almost in the same breath as his wondrous enthusiasm at God's splitting mountains to bring his people from afar, the prophet sees almighty God's love for His people as a mother's tender love for her child.

Today's gospel comes after the story of the paralyzed man at the pool of Bethsaida whom Jesus cured on the Sabbath. To the Jewish leaders' complaint that Jesus called God his Father, Jesus assured them of the equality between himself and the heavenly Father. Because Jesus had taken on human flesh, the Father had appointed him as people's judge. He judges justly, and will reward people according to the way they fulfill the Father's will. Jesus always did his Father's will, and by his word and example encourages us to do the same.

Jesus said that his heavenly Father's *works* convey a profound revelation. While the Sabbath commemorated God's rest after the creation, God is *ever* working — otherwise everything would crumble into nothing. Educated Jews knew that God's "rest" was only a figurative expression to mark the stability of the order which God had put into the world. God the Father works by keeping the created world in running condition, by bringing infants to birth, by calling others in death. Yet people allow themselves to be blind to the wonderful and the tender, and can become narrow and blinded. We can become immersed in red tape while the poor die of starvation, the handicapped are deprived of a full life, and the excitement of young people is smothered.

As with Isaiah speaking about the kingdom of Judah in exile, Jesus' ministry showed that God's power and tenderness is ongoing. It's the same with us. Our spiritual life continues to mature, with ups and downs. Were God to give power to the unprepared or immature, it would be like giving whiskey and car keys to teenage boys. The growing pains, crises, and periods of spiritual exile all indicate that the Lord isn't finished with us. Even when we die, God remains with us.

God never overpowers. God's power in this world is never the power of a muscle, a speed, a physical attractiveness, a brilliance, or a grace which makes you shout, "Yes! Yes! There is God!" The world's power tries to work that way, but God's power is more muted. It lies at a deeper level, at the ultimate base of things, and will, in the end, gently have the final say.

What does God's power look like? How does it feel to be God in this world? If you've ever been overpowered physically and been helpless, if you've ever been hit or slapped by someone and been powerless to defend yourself, then you've felt how God feels in this world. If you've ever dreamed a dream and found that your dream could never be realized, if you've cried tears and felt shame at your own inadequacy, then you've felt how God feels in this world. If you've ever been shamed in your enthusiasm and not been given a chance to explain yourself, if you've ever been cursed for your goodness by people who misunderstood you and you were powerless to make them see things your way, then you've felt how God feels in this world. If you've ever tried to make yourself attractive to someone and were incapable of it, if you've ever loved someone and wanted desperately to somehow make him or her notice you and found yourself hopelessly unable to do so, then you've felt how God feels in this world.

Not unlike the people of Judah in exile, many people live their lives of work, study, business, research, and social relationships separated from their faith. Without God's revelation, many have come to consider the world as an end in itself, with no reference to God. There's a disregard — more accurately, a fear and even terror — of anything that could cause suffering. With this outlook, words such as sin, cross, mortification, and eternal life become incomprehensible. The poor human being has become reduced to a stomach, sex organs, and a wallet.

Lent gives us an opportunity to know how to put the Christian stamp on our daily relationships with our family, among our neighbors, at our work, and in our leisure. This stamp consists of simplicity, sincerity, fidelity, meekness, generosity, solidarity, and joy.

As we prepare for Easter we can be conscious of the great joy that should be ours as we share with our neophytes their new life in Christ.

In today's first reading, Isaiah calls his period a time of favor. St. Paul takes this up and says simply, "Today is the favorable time, today is the day of salvation." He's right. Today is all we have: yesterday is gone, and perhaps we won't see tomorrow. Wherever we are spiritually, God is calling us to come nearer to Himself. And that's always today.

Jesus' Witnesses against Unbelief

As Jesus came closer to the end of his life, the issue between him and Jewish officialdom was coming to a head. Basically, that issue was whether he was truly God. In Jesus' controversy with the officials in today's gospel, anticipating his trial and death, he pointed to four key witnesses that bear testimony to his being God: St. John the Baptist, Jesus' own works, his heavenly Father, and the Scriptures.

As for *John,* while we call him "the Baptist," or "the Baptizer," he might with equal accuracy be called "the Witness": St. John the Evangelist says that he came to testify (1:7). The Baptist's testimony — always honest, humble, sincere, and direct — gives witness to many titles that can be given only to Jesus.

One title we might call "The Greater One": He's greater than I, said the Baptist, and he must increase while I must decrease. A second title under which the Baptist saw Jesus may be termed "The Vehicle of the Spirit." The Baptist recounted that, even before Jesus' baptism, God had told him that the one upon whom the Spirit would descend would himself be baptizing with the Holy Spirit. At Jesus' baptism, the Baptist saw the Spirit descend as a dove. A third title of the Baptist for Jesus is "God's Chosen One," an allusion to Isaiah, recognizing in Jesus the special Son of God, the chosen in whom the Father delights. But for the Baptist much of all that was hindsight, and it always troubled him that he hadn't immediately recognized Jesus.

Yet all these titles, though correct, can leave us relatively cold and unresponsive. But then, what image of Jesus might sufficiently open up human hearts? John's answer: a young, guiltless lamb frolicking in a field, before whom children laugh and adults grin. Jesus is, said John, the Lamb of God. This image con-

veys notes of innocence and fragility as well as whimsy and tenderness, and moves us to response.

As for the second witness, *Jesus' works,* we often lose sight
of the fact that the gospels constantly speak of the amazement
— the complete astonishment — of the crowds. The people's
testimony that he had done all things well alluded — probably
unconsciously — to God when He looked at all His creation and
called it good (Gn 1:31).

To take only one example, St. Peter had witnessed many
miracles of Jesus. He'd seen healings, including the cure of his
mother-in-law, but Peter didn't know medicine. He was present
when Jesus changed water into wine, but he wasn't a physicist.
But those miracles didn't reach him as much as the miraculous
number of fish the Apostles caught at Jesus' bidding did. He did
know fishing, and he could testify that what he had just experienced was extremely unusual, to say the least. When at the beginning of that incident Jesus had told Peter to put out into deep
water, Peter had called him "Master." Now, reflecting his awe,
he called him "Lord."

These kinds of works showed Jesus to be God. But to recognize a miracle — or a person — one must have an eye that
really sees. Many people had seen apples fall before Isaac Newton did, but Newton saw it and came up with the law of gravity;
many people had seen kettles of water boil before James Watt
did, but Watt saw it and came up with the steam engine.

The *heavenly Father,* too, gave testimony to Jesus' being God
and His Son. At Jesus' baptism, while the Holy Spirit appeared
in the form of a dove, the voice of the Father was heard. At Jesus'
transfiguration, his appearance was radically and beautifully
changed. Speaking with him were Moses, denoting Jesus as the
fruition of the Jewish Law, and Elijah, representing Jesus'
fulfillment of the testimony of the prophets.

As for the testimony of *the Scriptures* to Jesus' divinity, an
excellent example is in today's first reading. There Moses suc-

cessfully defended God's people; Jesus has done the same for us. Another example is the events that took place on the road to the little town of Emmaus, about seven miles from Jerusalem, after Jesus' crucifixion. Two disappointed disciples on the road away from Jerusalem met the risen Lord. Because he was resurrected — not resuscitated — and this was unique in all the history of the world, they didn't recognize him. His body was somewhat different from what they had seen when he walked the roads of the Holy Land. At first startled, the two disciples quickly recognized Jesus as they broke bread together. They were filled with joy, a proper consequence of meeting Jesus; if joy is absent, there's something amiss. A joyless Christian is a contradiction in terms.

Indeed, joy was characteristic of all the witnesses to the divinity of Jesus: John the Baptist, Jesus' works, the heavenly Father, and the Sacred Scriptures. During this second half of Lent, let's be joyful over whatever sacrifices we're able to make out of love, and let's remember in prayer those who have forgotten or neglected this period of grace.

We, too, are called to bear witness, to give testimony that Jesus is Lord in our lives. Our response is often like that of some of the characters in the Bible.

We can be like Peter, James, and John when Jesus took them up a high mountain and was transfigured. They were filled with fear. Also frightened, we look for excuses: "There must be someone else to do the job, someone better equipped, braver, smarter, more eloquent." God's reply is, "Yes, I know."

Abraham, chosen to be the father of the Jewish people, was called when he was old and childless. He gasped, "I'm 90 now. You'd better look for a younger man. I'm over the hill." God said, "Yes, I know."

When God appeared to Moses in the burning bush, he asked him to preach to Pharaoh. Moses replied, "I'm a man of poor speech. You know, when I'm under pressure, I stutter." God responded, "Yes, I know."

When God called Isaiah, he came up with an original excuse: "I can't say holy things. I have a dirty mouth." God said, "Yes, I know."

Jeremiah, the prophet, on hearing the call, said, "Oh no, not me, please. I can't be a spokesman for the Lord. I'm too young. They'll laugh at me." God said, "Yes, I know."

The prophet Jonah was called to convert the people of Nineveh, a mission to the "Big Apple" of those days, which he didn't want. So he fled before the face of the living God. Gobbled up by a large fish, he was taken to Nineveh, where God got His way anyhow.

The instinct to flee from God is so common that the English poet, Francis Thompson, wrote: "I fled him down the nights and down the days. / I fled him down the labyrinthine ways of my own mind."

That our call comes in ordinary ways doesn't make it any less authentic. God deserves and expects an answer.

Friday, Fourth Week of Lent
Ws 2:1, 12-22; Jn 7:1f.,10, 25-30

Evil People Have It in for Good People

In today's gospel, the plot of the wicked against Jesus was beginning to thicken. In the growing tension his opponents had many motives, some of them contemptible: prejudice, self-interest, politics, jealousy, hatred. Beneath all of these, the fundamental conflict was between the power of evil and the power of God —

between sin and grace — that was taking place during the life of Jesus and takes place in the life of each of us.

The last time Jesus was in Judea, four months before today's gospel, after he had cured the paralytic on a Sabbath day, Jewish officialdom had made up their minds to kill him. Even in the face of that, now it was time for Jesus to go up to the Holy City again. Jerusalem was the right place for his message — there he would find the elite of Israel.

The feast of Booths (or Tabernacles) was an opportunity. One of the three major Jewish feasts (besides Passover and Yom Kippur), it was celebrated during the month of Tishri (September-October). It commemorated the desert wanderings after the Exodus and was usually celebrated in booths (Hebrew *Succoth*). It was a very popular feast, often the occasion of national uprisings. Indeed, the feast may in addition have suggested to some of Jesus' followers the idea of a Messianic demonstration.

The Law of Moses said that every male over 13 living in Judea was obligated to present himself in Jerusalem for this feast. This year Jesus, because of the plots of the wicked against him, prudently decided to go privately after his disciples had gone. Upon his arrival some of the people recognized him just the same, and they wondered whether this was the man the officials wanted to kill. (The people of Jerusalem would be more aware of the officials' purpose than rural people might.)

Today's gospel is one of the most confrontational passages in the gospels, and shows how hatred by the Establishment leads inexorably to the arrest and death of Jesus. When some people said they knew him and his origins, Jesus replied that his earthly origin didn't prevent his having been sent by Him who has the right to "send" and with Whom he dwells. At this declaration some of the leaders, violently shocked, tried to seize him, but his hour hadn't yet come. The people whispered, still in fear of the officials who wouldn't give up their looking for ways to kill Jesus.

Hatred for goodness was the same when the Book of Wisdom was written at Alexandria in Egypt about a hundred years before Christ. The book wisely understands that without a belief in God true goodness isn't possible. Many people try to be good out of ideals that have no connection with God, but their principles wind up as less than satisfactory. The Book of Wisdom sets forth wicked peoples' erroneous philosophy of life. Their concept of life is completely this-worldly.

They resolve to plot against the good person. Why? Because his life and words are a reproach to them (vv. 12-16), and they determine to test the claims of the just man (vv. 17, 20). The just one is openly against their wicked doings, reproaches them, makes charges against them, tries to act as a person of God, bothers their conscience, rightly calls them debased, doesn't associate with their like, and calls the outcome of holy people happy.

To people of vice, virtuous people continue to be a hated provocation. The virtuous continue to be put down, ridiculed, and accused of hypocrisy, arrogance, condescension, and worse. Evil people can't stand people who try to be virtuous. No good deed goes unpunished. Among offenses to Jesus in our time are paintings featuring him on an obscene version of the cross, a depiction of a pope apparently engaging in a lewd act, and pages of a Bible defaced with Satanic marks. Many make fun of the Eucharist and Jesus' death on the cross. Some have compared confessionals to toilets. Priests have been called "sociopathic" and the celibacy vow "an empty sham." A New York radio station called the pope "a dirty old man walking around in a dress." In the art world, blasphemous art works intended to debase Christianity have routinely featured sex acts involving Jesus, or the pope, or priests.

All of this is treated solely as an issue of artistic freedom: the idea that in a free society, artists should be able to express themselves in any way they see fit. But these arguments are not applied consistently. The traditional passion plays have more or less disappeared because some people concluded they were anti-Semitic. The movie *The Birth of a Nation* has been banned from the Library of Congress's festival of the best films of the United States because of its sympathetic treatment of the Ku Klux Klan. Shakespeare's *Merchant of Venice* is rarely performed these days because of the sensitivity of the portrayal of Shylock as a Jew, and when it is performed the Shylock role is almost always altered to make him more sympathetic. No one would put a show on Broadway about scalp-collecting Indians or shuffling, happy black slaves. In the fight over the staging of a play called *Corpus Christi*, however, which depicted a gay Christ who had sexual relations with his Apostles, opponents were called "bigots."

It's refreshing to read the innocence and goodness of the homework assignment of an eight-year-old third-grade boy to explain God. He wrote:

"One of God's main jobs is making people. He doesn't make grown-ups, just babies. I think because they are smaller and easier to make.

"God's second most important job is listening to prayers. An awful lot of this goes on, since some people pray at times besides bedtime. God doesn't have time to listen to the radio or TV because of this. Because He hears everything there must be a terrible lot of noise in His ears, unless He has thought of a way to turn it off. You shouldn't go wasting God's time by going over your mom and dad's head asking for something they said you couldn't have.

"Atheists are people who don't believe in God. I don't think there are any who come to our church. Jesus used to do all the hard work like walking on water and performing miracles and trying to teach the people who didn't want to learn about God. They finally got tired of Him preaching to them and they crucified Him.

"His Dad (God) appreciated everything that he had done and all his hard work on earth so He told him he didn't have to go out on the road anymore, he could stay in heaven. So he did. And now he helps his Dad out by seeing things which are important for God to take care of and which ones he can take care of himself without having to bother God. Like a secretary only more important. You should always go to church on Sunday because it makes God happy, and if there's anybody you want to make happy, it's God. Don't skip church to do something you think will be more fun like going to the beach. This is wrong! And, besides, the sun doesn't come out at the beach until noon anyway.

"Your parents can't go everywhere with you, like to camp, but God can. It is good to know He's around you when you're scared in the dark or when you can't swim very good and you get thrown into real deep water by big kids. But you shouldn't just always think of what God can do for you. I figure God put me here and He can take me back anytime He pleases.

"And that's why I believe in God."

That leads to a further thought about good people versus bad. In a little Texas town, squirrels occupied the attics of the Presbyterian, Methodist, and Catholic churches along a street with big trees. The squirrels were a nuisance, chewing up the insulation and cutting the wires. Each congregation called a meeting to deal with the pests. The Presbyterians met first, but adjourned after an Elder pointed out that the squirrel invasion was preordained, and from a theological point of view there was nothing they should do about it. The Methodists met next, and a little old lady pleaded with the congregation to handle the problem in the gentle spirit of John Wesley, their founder. So the church bought a bunch of humane traps, took the squirrels to the edge of town, and turned them loose. By morning all the Methodist squirrels were back in their Methodist attic. The Catholics were the last to convene a meeting. The squirrels were quickly baptized into membership in the church, and now they come around only on Easter and Christmas.

Today gives rise to questions. Do we give enough attention to God's wisdom in order to make a good life, or are we satisfied with having enough street knowledge to make a living? Do we spend as much time through the week looking for wisdom as we do for the right television channel? Do we allow our selfish desires to be so strong that we can't pray properly? Do we have our baser nature in check so as to avoid any envy of good people?

Saturday, Fourth Week of Lent
Jr 11:18-20; Jn 7:40-53

No One Has Ever Spoken Like Jesus

When Jesus spoke, people listened — his enemies as well as his friends. The Temple cops whom the Pharisees had commanded to bring him in listened, too. As a result they didn't arrest him, as the Pharisees had commanded, because they were deeply moved by the fact that they'd never heard anyone speak like him (v. 46).

As for past scholars who had spoken and written, the cops who were in the secular tradition might have heard of some of the great Greek philosophers, from whom the Romans had inherited so much. The most important of these were Socrates, Plato, and Aristotle, all of whose works were concerned with the pursuit of wisdom.

Socrates had asked an important question: "What is a virtuous man, and what is a virtuous society?" Also, he said that the unexamined life is not worth living. Socrates had also posited the imperative "know thyself." And he had prayed that he might be beautiful within.

Yet, as the Temple cops ruminated, Socrates had never spoken as Jesus did.

For Plato, the arts — music and poetry and dancing, and even architecture — at their best are indispensable means of character education. Also in Plato are arguments for survival after death. And Plato had posited a "cascade of creation." In a waterfall from the Form of the Good came manifestations which are three in number but are really all one: goodness, truth, and beauty. Each of these three in turn produces other forms. Goodness, for example, produces such forms as wisdom, courage, and temperance, which in turn produce yet other forms, cascading further down to our world of appearances.

How we come to a knowledge of the world of ideas is explained in Plato's most important allegory, that of the cave. Human beings are chained in a cave, their backs to the entrance, facing the cave's rear wall. Outside the entrance, the sun (the Form of the Good) shines. In front of the mouth of the cave is the world of forms or ideas, whose shadows are reflected on the cave's rear wall. It's only those shadows that ordinary people see. The object of life is to free ourselves from our chains, escape outside the cave into the sun, and turn around to the world of ideas (conversion).

However, as the Temple cops experienced, Plato was no Jesus.

The thought of Aristotle — philosopher, logician, and scientist — perhaps more than any other thinker has characterized the orientation and content of all that is termed Western civilization. He tutored the future Alexander the Great. He opened the Lyceum, an institution of higher learning as a center for speculation and research that rivaled Plato's Academy. He wrote tracts on logic, the philosophy of nature, psychology, metaphysics, ethics, politics, law, religious philosophy, art, and rhetoric.

In art theory, he wrote on comedy, literary criticism, music, poetry, style, and tragedy. His *Poetics* gave a foundation for the critical investigation of literature. His theory of *catharsis* said that, in our daily lives, some emotions are generated which we would be better off without and which we should try to dispel; art is the agency that helps us to do that.

A most frequently-cited concept of truth is Aristotle's definition of it as "the adequation of intellect and thing." Although denied in Jesus' time by the likes of Pilate and in ours by the likes of currently dominant Positivist theory, Aristotle's definition of truth makes logical discourse possible. All in all, Aristotle's tradition has continued without interruption from his death in 322 B.C. to the present.

But, as the Temple cops knew, even Aristotle's lofty teachings were no match for the teachings of Jesus.

The idea of cognitive moral development, too, went back at least as far as these ancient greats. Aristotle's discussions of "what is the good for man?" were relevant in Jesus' time, and remain relevant today. Aristotle also saw the need for goals in life. He said that "to a ship without a destination, no wind is favorable." The importance of that is recognized today even by such as Yogi Berra, who is alleged to have said, "You got to be very careful if you don't know where you're going, because you might not get there."

Then, too, the Pharisees' guards might have heard of the discussions of the nature of the good life. Aristotle inclined toward defining the good life as a life of thought, the Roman Cicero toward service to the State, and for the Greek Epicurus the good life was a life of personal pleasure.

The cops who refused to take Jesus in because no one had ever spoken like him would be more likely to have been familiar with their own Jewish Scriptures' pursuit of wisdom. Five books in the Jewish Scriptures are usually classified as "wisdom literature": Proverbs, Job, Ecclesiastes, Sirach, and Wisdom. About three-fourths of the approximately 400 occurrences of the word "wisdom" in the Old Testament appear in these five books. Wisdom is present also in the counsels in Tobit (4:3-21 and 12:6-13) and the poem in Baruch (3:9-4:4), as well as in other books of the Jewish Scriptures.

Wisdom, this noblest exercise of a human being's intellectual faculties and moral qualities whereby a person attains a greater degree of knowledge or understanding, in the Bible isn't usually a theoretical virtue but a practical knowledge. Yet it strives for a moral end: It's a means toward living in harmony with God's holy will. Because wisdom is a precious gift of God, the Jewish Scriptures said that people should pray for it constantly, prepare their soul for receiving it, and work hard to pursue it. The Pharisees' Temple cops may have heard that, as a result of prayer, King Solomon had received the gift of wisdom.

Yet the Temple cops perceived that none of these wise men, poets, and scholars had ever spoken like Jesus.

Jesus' words called for people to live in a spirit of love and forgiveness. The cops had previously been told by the Pharisees that the way to holiness was to observe many external laws. These were both numerous and difficult to understand, and the Pharisees made a good living providing interpretations of them. The Pharisees rejected Jesus because he gave people more personal control over their lives, and he reduced their many laws to two that even these cops could understand: love God truly, and honestly identify and love your neighbor.

Jeremiah's image in today's first reading of the trustful lamb led to slaughter would ultimately be Jesus' lot. John the Baptist had pointed out Jesus as the Lamb of God who takes away our sins. Jesus as the Suffering Servant in Isaiah bears the sins of the multitude as he allows himself to be silently led to the cross. The Paschal Lamb of the Passover recalls the people's liberation from slavery into freedom.

The Pharisees, and their modern counterparts, seem not to

believe that Jesus is the Messiah because he just didn't have the right home address! That's hardly a good excuse in our modern democratic tradition, which holds that famous people make a birthplace famous rather than a place of birth making a person famous.

The coming last two weeks of Lent are a prime time for us to examine some of our individual excuses for not quite completely believing Jesus and his teaching, for not loving and serving him with all our heart and soul and mind and strength.

Monday, Fifth Week of Lent

Dn 13:1-9,15-17, 19-30, 33-62 (or 13:41-62); Jn 8:1-11

Look Up to Heaven!

The Hebrew word corresponding to the name "Susanna" is the name of a flower that is traditionally translated as "lily." Her story in the Book of Daniel is one folk tale among many to illustrate morality. She had been falsely accused by judges whose minds weren't on true judgments but on the satisfaction of their lust. She was saved in the nick of time by the clever cross-examination of the prophet Daniel.

Superficially, at least, the primary purpose of the story is to show that virtue (here in the form of chastity) triumphs with God's help over vice (here in the form of lust and deceit). While even on that level the story is valuable, some exegetes have seen deeper meanings. For them the two wicked elders symbolize the pagans and the apostate Jews, especially at the time of King Antiochus IV Epiphanes, who tried to make the Jews, here symbolized by Susanna, fall into the sin of apostasy from Yahweh —

a sin that the prophets often called fornication and adultery.

A key that cuts through the story lies in one line that says Susanna through her tears looked up to heaven, for she trusted in the Lord wholeheartedly (v. 35). By contrast, her two wicked accusers suppressed their consciences; they wouldn't allow their eyes to look to heaven (v. 9). You can turn off your conscience. Pol Pot, leader of a Cambodian regime that killed perhaps more than a million people, said he slept well at night. In an interview, he said he came to "carry out the struggle." In South Africa, where officials were engaged in apartheid, one minister testified that when the Cabinet approved plans to "eliminate," "neutralize," or "permanently remove from society" political opponents, no one was suggesting that anyone be killed. The phrases are reminiscent of Nazi euphemisms, which referred to the murder of Jews as "the final solution," "evacuation," or "special treatment." In Latin America, many sophisticated people blinded themselves to dictators' crimes because they were getting rich.

When we fix our eyes on heaven, we allow ourselves to be wholly absorbed in God and from this we acquire an exceptional peace and firm strength. This inner peace begets many other admirable qualities, too. Susanna had a spirit of patience, for example, whereby she didn't lash out angrily against her accusers or turn in panic to her own defense. Conduct like hers also begets honor, serenity, and forgiveness. Possessing the strength and integrity that derived from her inner peace, she prayed to God who, she said, knows what is hidden and is aware of all things (v. 42).

Today's gospel complements and contrasts with the story of Susanna. Jesus was in the Temple, after the Feast of Tabernacles. This autumn and thanksgiving feast marked the end of the fruit harvest. During the entire week the Israelites had also to dwell in outdoor tents or booths of tree twigs, to remind them of the time when their ancestors lived in tents after their departure from Egypt.

An angry crowd brought to Jesus a woman who had been caught in adultery. There's a striking parallel with the similar incident in today's reading from the Book of Daniel. In both stories, a woman, threatened by a crowd, is saved because one person intervenes and alters things. The stories, however, end very differently: one in peace and the other in violence. At the end of Susanna's story, Daniel turned the crowd against the woman's accusers, demanding their deaths by stoning, and the crowd, in a frenzy of emotion, obliged.

In the gospel story, Jesus calmly backed down the accusers of the woman caught in adultery. Unlike Susanna, this woman was guilty, but that was incidental to what was happening. Like Susanna, the adulterous woman before Jesus was there because of jealousy and mob frenzy. And Jesus, like Daniel, confronted the crowd. His protest to the crowd was more penetrating in conscience than was Daniel's — let the one who is without sin cast the first stone — and it also had a very different effect. The woman was saved, but what followed was the exact opposite of mob-scene hysteria. Jesus' words not only saved a woman, but defused a potential explosion. Nobody died, and instead everyone went home more attuned to humility and truth. Jesus is the ultimate example of the nonviolent peacemaker.

From this story of Jesus some people have gotten the impression that Jesus was soft on sins of sex. People think of his reaction to this woman caught in adultery, and another story of a sinful woman (Lk 7:36-50), and his conduct with the Samaritan woman who had many husbands (Jn 4). Today's story suggests that Jesus did modify the Mosaic Law on one point: sexual immorality shouldn't incur a death penalty from the state. This wasn't because sex didn't matter to him, but rather because stoning was a terminal act that didn't give opportunity for repentance and reform.

Moreover, all these stories confirm what we know about Jesus elsewhere: that he aggressively sought the lost, ate with them, and fraternized with them. But the same Jesus who could protect an adulterous woman from stoning also took a very strong stance on divorce and remarriage. We don't conclude from Jesus' outreach to tax collectors that he was soft on economic exploitation. Why, then, do some conclude from his outreach to sexual sinners that sexual sin wasn't so important to Jesus?

There's no historical basis, either, for arguing that Jesus might have been neutral toward same-sex intercourse. There's overwhelming evidence that Jesus would have strongly opposed same-sex intercourse had such behavior been a serious problem among first-century Jews.

First, Jesus' "silence" has to be set against the backdrop of unequivocal and strong opposition to same-sex intercourse in the Hebrew Bible and throughout early Judaism. It's unlikely that Jesus would have overturned the prohibition of the Mosaic Law on a strongly-held moral matter such as this; Jesus wasn't shy about disagreeing with prevailing viewpoints.

Second, the notion of Jesus' "silence" has to be qualified. According to the gospel of St. Mark (7:21-23) Jesus spoke out against *porneia* (sexual immorality) and accepted the Decalogue commandment against adultery (Mk 10:19). In Jesus' day, and for many centuries thereafter, *porneia* was universally understood in Judaism to include same-sex intercourse. Moreover, the Decalogue commandment against adultery was treated as a broad rubric prohibiting all forms of sexual practice that deviated from the creation model in Chapters 1 and 2 in the Book of Genesis, including homoerotic intercourse.

Third, that Jesus held high the male-female model for sexual relationships in Genesis as the basis for defining God's will for sexuality is obvious from his back-to-back citation (Mk 10:6f.) that God made us male and female (Gn 1:27) and that for this reason a man shall leave his father and mother and be joined to his wife, and the two shall become one flesh (Gn 2:24).

In our age of "tolerance," we should love all people. Let's

remember, though, that love is a much better, and far more scriptural, concept than tolerance. If we really love someone, we won't provide approval, let alone cultural incentives, for forms of behavior that are self-destructive and other-destructive. Jesus combined an intensification of God's ethical demand in the areas of sex and money with an active and loving outreach to sexual sinners and economic exploiters. We should do the same. Love the sinner, hate the sin.

Tuesday, Fifth Week of Lent
Nb 21:4-9; Jn 8:21-30

The Cross in Perspective

Many of our Jewish brethren look upon the cross and can't stand it. To them it represents centuries of oppression from a society formed mostly by Christians: ghettos, pogroms, inquisitions, name-calling like "Christ killers," murders. Sadly, many of these atrocities were done in the name of the cross. Some pagans still look upon the cross and the sacrifice it represents as foolishness, as St. Paul said long ago. Many people of good will look at the cross and feel compassion for Jesus' pain. Many Christians see it as an overwhelming cause for sadness; some find it a source of joy in Jesus' love.

The position we should take is portended in today's first reading — the story that begins with the early Hebrews going through the desert and being bitten by poisonous snakes. The snakes were called saraphs, Hebrew probably for "the fiery one," from the burning effect of their poisonous bite. As a result of Moses' prayer, the Lord told him to make a bronze saraph and mount it on a pole, and if anyone who had been bitten looked at it, he would recover. Moses did as instructed, with the promised results.

Jesus applied that picture to himself when he told Nicodemus that just as Moses lifted up the serpent in the desert, so must he be lifted up, so that everyone who believes in him may have eternal life (Jn 3:14f). The saraph, mounted on the pole as in today's first reading, released those doomed to die. Jesus, lifted on the cross, saves us from spiritual death.

Jesus refers to it in today's gospel, in which his statements move his conversation with the Pharisees to a higher level at each turn. He finally tells the Pharisees that when they lift up the Son of Man, then they will realize that he is, as he said, I AM — that is, God (v. 28). He addressed this final appeal to some among his audience who were animated by a sincere desire to follow the way shown by God. For Christians, the cross is especially important. It represents the way God's Son died for all the human race.

The world in which Jesus was crucified was a world of unrelenting cruelty. Who today could imagine, much less condone, the sight of men and women being fed to beasts as spectators shrieked their delight? To the Romans, the spectacle was a just punishment for lawbreakers. What's to be made of a superpower like Rome that conquered cities by enslaving the men and killing the women and children? Owning or killing people, Romans believed, was as natural as water running downhill. Who can comprehend a father tossing an infant into the village dung heap for being female, sick, or a surplus mouth to feed?

In the arena, the afternoon brought variety. Some of the captive men, trained and equipped with spears, lived to fight another day. But for others, the outcome was never in doubt. They were the *bestiarii* — condemned criminals who later would include Christian men and women — thrown into the arena with no weapons. The carnivore often was a quick-killing lion; many fans preferred smaller beasts that did more dragging and tearing. By the time of Christ, centuries of rough existence had bred a Roman acceptance of savagery and the conviction that life was a series of bleak choices.

Although today the cross is one of the most widely used symbols of Christianity, it was almost never used as a religious symbol by early Christians. In early Christianity, the cross was still being used for crucifixion and torture. To wear it around one's neck would be like wearing a miniature electric chair around your neck today.

In addition, early Christians were reluctant to use such a symbol of disgrace for their budding religion. They were safer using more subtle signs. Their symbols were such as the fish, whose letters in Greek spelled out "Jesus Christ God's Son Savior"; the anchor as a sign of hope in Christ; and various forms of christograms — for example, the first letters of the word "Christ" in Greek superimposed on one another, like "Chi Rho."

Nevertheless, the Church fathers spoke very strongly of the value of the cross, and this sign became more public after Roman Emperor Constantine. His conversion to Christianity in the fourth century put an end to crucifixion in the Roman Empire. It took another two centuries to put a figure on images of the cross.

Throughout the centuries, Christians have recognized the snakes around them that are potentially fatal to their spirit — worldliness, pride, indifference, coldness. They've knelt before the cross of suffering in all times of need and distress. The cross has been held before the eyes of those facing death. It has led missionary journeys so that those who looked upon it might have new life. Christ lifted up on the cross is the image which identifies his followers in every culture. The one symbol that captures everything about Jesus is the crucifix — the cross with Jesus' body on it. The crucifix contains a great deal about humankind and about God, a great deal about love and about hate, much about sin and about grace. We remember all this as we prepare to celebrate its veneration, especially on Good Friday.

Why, in our cruel times when individuals are tortured and masses of people are exterminated, do we pay tribute to a man who, millennia ago, was crucified? The answer is twofold. First, Jesus Christ is God. Secondly, time, too, is a cross. For us, time is horizontal — that is to say, our watches tick away one second after another, today follows yesterday, this month comes before next month, this year is sandwiched between last year and next year, and so on. For God, though, time is vertical — that is, all time is simultaneously present together at every instant. As Jesus says in today's gospel, I AM. That means that not only is Jesus' crucifixion present to him today, but our role in it is also present.

What is our role like? Am I like Judas, who betrays him? Like Peter, who at this point doesn't meet the test of love? Like the leaders of the people, who feel threatened by him? Like Caiaphas, who is self-serving toward him? Like Pilate, who is weak and pragmatic toward him? Like Pilate's wife, who is superstitious about him? Like the crowd, who knew so little about him that they allowed themselves to be manipulated about him? Like Simon the Cyrenean, who took up Jesus' cross because he was forced to? Like the Roman centurion, who finally recognized him as God?

The best test is whether in our daily attitudes and actions we're faithful to Christian principles: principles of justice, of peace, of love, of human existence.

Truth, Freedom, and Independence

When in today's gospel Jesus spoke to the leaders of the people, he told them that those who remained in his word would come to know the truth, and the truth would set them free (v. 32).

Truth and freedom! One complication is their meaning. How can truth make you free? A poster reads, "The truth shall make you free — but first it will make you miserable!" The truth does sometimes make us miserable, all the more as we cling to cherished illusions about ourselves. But that misery is temporary; the truth *does* ultimately make us free. It can give insights into ourselves, the world, and God that will enable us to escape our bonds and become all that God meant us to be.

Pilate would later ask Jesus, "What is truth?" That Roman pragmatist and his modern descendants would say that truth is whatever you can use for your own advantage. Others say that truth is something personal and therefore relative. Still others say that truth is always only a scientific "warranted assertion" — that is, for the present. It's always changing.

To teach values, a college teacher used a short story about a small American farm town where one person was killed each year to make the crops grow. In the story, a woman was ritually stoned to death by her husband, her 12-year-old daughter, and her 4-year-old son. A class discussion of human sacrifice yielded no moral comments, even under persistent questioning. One male student said the ritual killing in the story "almost seems a need." Asked if she believed in human sacrifice, a female student said, "I really don't know. It was a religion of long standing...." This was a woman who wrote passionately of saving the whales, of concern for the rain forests, and of her tender care of a stray dog.

Ten to twenty percent of college students deplore what the

Nazis did, but their disapproval is expressed as a matter of taste or personal preference, not moral judgment. Overdosing on nonjudgmentalism is a growing problem in schools and colleges. Some students are unwilling to oppose large moral horrors, including human sacrifice, ethnic cleansing, and slavery, because they think that no one has the right to criticize the moral views of another person, group, or culture.

Multiculturalism has probably played a role in spreading nonjudgmentalism. A nurse says she teaches a course for her hospital personnel in multicultural understanding, and if something is part of a person's culture, we ought not judge. Many students often think they are so locked into their own group perspectives of ethnicity, race, and gender that moral judgment is impossible, even in the face of great evils.

Students often say flatly that treating humans as superior to dogs and rodents is immoral. Moral shrugging may be on the rise, but old-fashioned and rigorous moral criticism is alive and well on certain selected issues: smoking, environmentalism, women's rights, animal rights.

Some students come to college dogmatically committed to a moral relativism that offers them no grounds to think about cheating, stealing, and other moral issues. It's "absolutophobia" — the unwillingness to say that some behavior is just plain wrong. This is fed into by modern theory on campuses that denies the existence of any objective truth: all we can have are clashing perspectives. Intellectual laziness and the simple fear of unpleasantness are factors. "Values clarification" programs, which say that teachers shouldn't indoctrinate other peoples' children and that values emerge as personal preferences, are now giving way to "character education." The search is on for a teachable consensus rooted in simple decency and respect. One American philosopher, however, wrote that the highest duty is to search for truth with unbiased minds, and the highest courage is to follow the truth always and everywhere regardless of where it may lead us.

Those who believe in Jesus' kind of truth would say that truth is what corresponds between the mind and reality; it's therefore objective, binding on all, constant, absolute, and unchanging. The truth, understood in that way, will make you free.

And what is freedom? Our nation was founded in behalf of "life, liberty, and the pursuit of happiness." Our Constitution's First Amendment contains a clause guaranteeing the "free exercise" of religion. President Lincoln's Gettysburg Address called for "a new birth of freedom." Many in our country pride themselves in expressing freedom of choice — which they grant for abortion, but not for parents who want a non-government school for their children. And we speak of "the free world" in contradistinction to so much of the world that's enslaved by politics or empty stomachs. Christianity asserts that freedom means the right and the ability to do what we *ought* — which doesn't necessarily always mean a universal right to what we *want*.

Does the truth making us free entail independence? The United States has a Declaration of Independence, and every year celebrates Independence Day. Independence is great! We all want it. Yet there's another side we must learn if we're to be truly free. The signers of the Declaration of Independence discovered their strength by *depending* on one another. The words "one another" are found in over a hundred verses of the New Testament. We discover true freedom when we learn to be *interdependent*.

In today's gospel, all of these considerations were beyond the thinking of Jesus' audience. They took complaisant pride more in their being the descendants of Abraham (v. 33) and in stating that they had never been enslaved to anyone. They wouldn't be so impudent as to deny that Israel had been enslaved by Assyrians, Babylonians, Persians, and Macedonians, and was now vassal to the Romans. What they meant was that, whatever their past sad history, since their return from Babylon they had never bowed before strange gods.

Jesus corrected them (vv. 34-36) on two points. First, despite what they said, they were in reality sinners and the slaves of sin. This was the implication of even their precious Mosaic Law with its unending rites of purification. Secondly, said Jesus, although they were *physical* descendants of Abraham, true faith isn't in the genes.

Then Jesus tore the veil from what they had kept hidden, by telling them twice the truth. They were trying to kill him. While still claiming Abraham as their father, they denied that Jesus was doing the works of the heavenly Father. Jesus (v. 41) in turn accused them of doing the works of *their* father, the devil.

Today's reading from the Book of Daniel presents us with models of devotion to truth and the proper use of freedom. It's the story of three young civil servants: in Hebrew their names were Hananiah, Azariah, and Mishael; in Babylonian they were called Shadrach, Meshach, and Abednego. The Babylonian King Nebuchadnezzar was a particularly vicious conqueror. As only one example, before he blinded the Jewish King Hezekiah he had Hezekiah's son killed before his father's eyes, so that that would be the last sight Hezekiah would remember.

Nebuchadnezzar built a ninety-foot idol and required everyone to worship it whenever his band played a certain song. On today's occasion, when the tune was finished everyone knelt except the three Jewish civil servants. Nebuchadnezzar, in a furious rage, condemned them to be burned to death. They had exercised their freedom; their commitment to the truth of their faith had been absolute. Only after that commitment in the deadly fire were they protected by an angel of God. The prayer of the three young men in the furnace is one of the most powerful prayers of the Old Testament, and forms a fitting commentary on today's reading. They prayed that, whether they burned to death or were saved, may God's will be done, and they would serve no other god.

Over and over Jesus offers us real truth and true freedom. We can lose freedom by way of habits, prejudices, sins, and illusions. Being reared as a Catholic isn't our whole story. At some point, we have to make an adult act of faith. Lent is a time to examine how deeply we have made that faith our own, along with its foundations of truth, freedom, and independence.

Thursday, Fifth Week of Lent
Gn 17:3-9; Jn 8:51-59

Keep the Faith!

A lot depends on our point of view. A humorous modern example was Rosencrantz the haberdasher. When he returned from a visit to Rome, his partner in his men's clothing store hung on his every word of describing his experiences. "I was even in a group that went to the Vatican," said Rosencrantz proudly, "where we were blessed by the Pope."

"The Pope!" exclaimed his partner. "What does he look like?"

"A very pious man, spiritual, almost saintly," said Rosencrantz. "I figure a size thirty-eight short."

Jesus' conversation with officialdom in today's gospel opens (v. 51) with Jesus, perceiving that they were spiritually dead, promising them once more the gift of immortal spiritual life for whomever abides by his word. The officials, increasingly uncomfortable with this concern with *spiritual* realities, changed their point of view to a *material* one. They seized on Jesus' allusion to Abraham and tried to put Jesus in a difficult position with regard to Abraham and the prophets (v. 52).

Jesus replied by saying that the Pharisees didn't know God (v. 55), using "know" in their sense of a practical knowledge manifest in conduct, almost equivalent to "love." Because the rabbis taught that God had revealed the future to Abraham, Jesus identified himself with Abraham's vision (v. 56).

As always in St. John's gospel, the leaders spoke to the surface level. They discussed chronological age (v. 57). Abraham was long dead, yet Jesus was claiming to give eternal life in a way superior to anything that their precious Abraham ever had.

The name of Abraham occurs more than three hundred times in the Bible, nine of them in today's Scripture readings alone. He's for the Jewish people a pioneer and paragon of faith, hope, and love of the God who was thenceforth identified as the God of Abraham. No wonder they bristled at Jesus' mention of him. What kind of arrogant nonsense was Jesus speaking? Abraham the greatest was dead; was Jesus claiming to be greater than he?

Arrogant nonsense? Actually, it was Jesus' enemies who were arrogant. How can smart people be so arrogant? Well, well-educated people are particularly susceptible to four fallacies, precisely because they *are* so skilled: the egocentrism fallacy, whereby they come to believe that the world revolves, or at least should revolve, around them; the omniscience fallacy, whereby they come to believe that they know all there is to know and therefore don't have to listen to the advice of others; the omnipotence fallacy, whereby they come to believe that their brains and education somehow make them all-powerful; and the invulnerability fallacy, whereby they come to believe not only that they can do what they want, but that others will never be clever enough to figure out what they've been up to or to get back at them. Of course, many more people than the Pharisees are arrogant.

When Jesus said "before Abraham came to be, I AM" (v. 58), he was referring to the name God revealed to Moses when the latter asked His name (Ex 3:13f.). Jesus' hearers knew exactly what he meant. This was one of the most striking of all Jesus' affirmations about himself, and one which drew the anger of the leaders. Notice that Jesus didn't escape by his divine power or by a miracle: he hid himself. So while the gospel prompts us to contemplate Jesus as "the word from the beginning," long before Abraham, it also reminds us that our faith doesn't deliver us from having to use all means which are at hand during life to keep the message of faith alive.

Jesus' assertion, if not true, would be blasphemous. He's applying the name of God (Yahweh, which means I AM) to himself in the clearest and most direct identification possible of himself with God. Out of frustration, the leaders wanted to kill him (v. 59).

Abraham, who appears in both of today's readings, is for Jews their "founding father"; for Muslims a "friend of God," their patriarch; and for Christians a model of faith. God put Abraham to many tests. The first recorded was when God appeared to the aged Abram (his name before his covenant with God) in his home town of Haran in Mesopotamia (now Iraq) to tell him to travel to Canaan to fulfill the destiny God had in mind for him there. Although the possessions of this nomad weren't many, it's not difficult for us to imagine his hardships in having to leave his home, his extended family, and all the things that made up his world, to face the perils and uncertainty of the unknown. But Abram lived his life searching for God's voice; being a good man, when he heard it he took the risk of letting go of all that was secure and familiar to journey by faith into the completely unknown.

Because of his faithfulness, God entered a covenant with him, the sign of which is circumcision. It seems that circumcision may be related to human sacrifice, which was widespread in some ancient Mideast cultures (including, at some periods, the Jews) as a way of placating and supplicating the gods. Circumcision may take the place of human sacrifice. A part of the body is substituted for the whole. Because an intimate relationship was seen between individuals and the entire community or tribe, circumcision, involving the foreskin of the male organ of procreation, proclaimed that the whole nation, the whole clan, present and future, was consecrated to the god it worshiped.

It was at that point, as today's first reading says, that his name was changed from Abram to Abraham. For the ancient Israelites, a change of name often denoted a change of relationship with God: the person was considered to be getting a fresh start. The New Testament often followed the same procedure: Saul's name was changed to Paul, Levi's to Matthew, Simon's to Peter.

Abraham is our model in faith. He believed in a God who can make the impossible possible and who encourages people to *dare* — to dare *anything*. Years ago there was a group of brilliant young men at the University of Wisconsin who seemed to have great creative literary talent. They were would-be poets, novelists, and essayists. These promising young men met regularly to critique each others' work. They were heartless, tough, and even mean in their criticism. The sessions became such periods of criticism that the members of this exclusive club called themselves the "Stranglers."

Not to be outdone, the women of literary talent at the university were determined to start a club of their own, comparable to the Stranglers. They called themselves the "Wranglers." They, too, read their works to one another. But there was one great difference. Their criticism was much more positive, more encouraging.

Twenty years later an alumnus of the university did an exhaustive study in which he noticed a vast difference in the accomplishments of the Stranglers as opposed to the Wranglers. Not one of the bright young men from the Stranglers had achieved a significant literary accomplishment. From the Wranglers, though, had come six or more successful writers, some of national renown.

The talent between the two was probably the same, as was the level of education. But the Stranglers strangled, while the Wranglers were determined to give each other a lift. The Stranglers advanced self-doubt, the Wranglers encouragement.

Abraham's belief foreshadowed the Christian's belief in Jesus. Especially as we approach the scandal of Holy Week, we should imitate the constancy and the encouragement of Abraham's faith.

Friday, Fifth Week of Lent

Jr 20:10-13; Jn 10:31-42

What's Your Relationship to Your God?

A small boy once approached his older sister with a question: "Susie, can anybody ever really see God?" Busy with other things, Susie curtly replied, "No, of course not, silly. God is so far up in heaven that nobody can see Him."

After a time in which the question still bothered him, he approached his mother: "Mom, can anybody ever really see God?" "No," she said gently, "God is a spirit, and He dwells in our hearts, but we can't really see Him."

Not long afterwards, his old grandfather took the boy on a fishing trip. They were having a great time when the sun was beginning to set and the grandfather stared silently at the exquisite beauty before them. On seeing the face of his grandfather reflecting such deep peace and contentment, the boy spoke hesitantly, "Grandpa, I wasn't going to ask anybody else — but I wonder if you can answer a question I've been wondering about

a long time. Can anybody — can anybody — ever really see
God?"

The old man didn't even turn his head. A long moment
passed before he finally answered quietly, "Son, it's getting so that
I can't see anything else."

Both Jeremiah and Jesus brought God too close for comfort for those who thought they had an inside track to Him. In
the first reading, Jeremiah rocked then-current theological foundations by criticizing the popular belief, which came to understand God's covenant with David as an unseen protective shield
for "the chosen people." Jeremiah insisted that the covenant was
not an automatic key to salvation, but a mutual obligation: upon
people as well as God. Jeremiah also provided a foretaste of what
Jesus would suffer at the hands of the wicked. The sensitive
Jeremiah, who had never wanted to be a prophet, knew these
conflicts when he preached and suffered in Jerusalem before the
Jews' sixth-century captivity.

For Jeremiah's speaking out in God's behalf, he was de-
nounced and put in prison. Faithfulness to his mission brought
him nothing but heartbreak. His former friends sided with his
enemies. He knew the whispers of many. They had made several attempts on his life. They were watching for any misstep so
that they could take revenge. Feeling alone, betrayed, discouraged, and abandoned even by God, he experienced anger against
his persecutors.

He had a most sensitive understanding of God's love for His
people and the bonds of love and loyalty that should exist between people and their God. In the heart-rending words of today's
first reading, in the middle of all the strong contradictions,
Jeremiah on trial kept faith in Yahweh's promises and knew that
the Lord was with him (v. 11). He began this passage with his
feelings about being an outcast, a stranger to his brothers, and
insulted by many; at the same time at the end of the passage he
expressed his desire to praise God.

By Jesus' time seven centuries later, the Jewish people had come to see God as majestic and remote. The comfort in that was that, with God so distant, people could justify themselves in not living according to His will. Jesus insisted that God is indeed majestic, but not remote. The implication of that is that everything in our lives, what is called "sacred" and what is secular, has spiritual — and therefore eternal — ramifications. There's a spiritual dimension to every aspect of ordinary life.

In today's gospel passage, Jesus was in Jerusalem for the Feast of Lights. Falling in mid-December, this feast commemorated the consecration (*chanukah*) of the Temple in 165 B.C., after its profanation by the pagan King Antiochus IV Epiphanes. The celebration lasted eight days, during which there were splendid lighting displays and large gatherings of people. It was *the* feast of Jewish nationalism, but wasn't prescribed by the Mosaic Law like the great feasts of Passover, Pentecost, and Tabernacles. Because of the weather Jesus was in Solomon's Porch of the Temple, as he walked and talked. His going back across the Jordan (v. 40) wasn't a hurried trip, but a missionary journey.

The religious authorities were agitated by his attitudes to the Mosaic Law and to the Temple. Also antagonizing them was his keeping company with tax collectors and sinners. But it was especially irritating when he insisted that his mercy toward sinners was God's attitude, and when he forgave sins they were horrified at what seemed to them to be blasphemy. His final claim of divine identity was too much for them.

Then as now, in the face of idolatry and social injustice many people don't want religion to go out of the sanctuary. What, they ask, does religion have to do with daily life? Though we have the motto "In God We Trust" on our money and we have God's name in our pledge to the flag, many don't trust in God in any meaningful way; and, sad to say, many interpret the separation of church and state to mean separation of religion from the people and morals from the country.

How did the First Amendment of the United States Constitution about the non-establishment of religion become equated
with language that appears nowhere in the Constitution: "the wall
of separation of church and state"? It's well known that Thomas
Jefferson, in an 1802 letter to the Danbury Baptist Association
in Connecticut, used that phrase. It's less well known that the
Danbury Baptists, who had written Jefferson in hopes of getting
ammunition to use in their battle against laws favoring the state's
Congregationalist majority, quietly shelved the presidential mis-
sive.

The metaphor of separation, let alone a *wall* of separation,
suggested a distance, a lack of contact, an incompatibility, even
an antagonism, between religion and government. How did
church-state separation become virtually synonymous with religious freedom? Well, by mid-nineteenth century, many Ameri-
cans were in full-blown rebellion not against religion as such but
against church structures and authorities. This attitude, it so
happened, converged with the nativist anti-Catholicism. True
religion was for them individual and antidogmatic, independent
not just of state pressures but of church pressures, too.

And the Ku Klux Klan made separation of church and state
a central element in its anti-Catholicism. The Klan exerted profound political power and, probably more than any other national
group at that time, drew United States citizens to the principle
of separation.

Eventually, openly anti-Christian secularists insisted that
genuine separation should rule out chaplains in legislatures, prisons, and the armed forces; bar Bible reading in schools; require
taxation of church property; repeal laws forbidding Sunday com-
merce; and so on. Interestingly, at first the secularists didn't claim
to find this thoroughgoing separation in the First Amendment,
but, with allies like President Ulysses S. Grant, they campaigned
in the 1870's for separation.

Of course, keeping politics, especially vehement politics, out of the pulpit may be a sound idea. Separation may offer a plausible legal solution to a wide range of issues. Separation of church and state, but not of religion and citizenry, nor of God and people, has both simplified and impoverished discussions of religious liberty in ways that obscure the necessarily complex relationships between civil and religious authorities.

Today some people wish they'd never heard of sin or responsibility or fear of the Lord; they think their lives would be a lot more fun without them. In the long run, though, we're down-deep happier when we've done the right thing. Humble meditation on today's truths will hopefully bring together reverence and awe before the Lord such that, like responsive children, we place our confidence in God.

In a little more than a week, Lent will be over. There's still time to ask ourselves two questions. During this Lent, have we yet come to a greater discernment of who God is for us? Have we found in ourselves some previously unknown area of darkness to be avoided and of unexpected light to be encouraged?

Saturday, Fifth Week of Lent
Ezk 37:21-28; Jn 11:45-57

A Chosen People

What a contrast between God's proposed plan through Ezekiel in today's first reading and the one which Jesus' enemies — leaders of the people — put together in the gospel! God's plan in Ezekiel is positive: the return of the people to their own land after an era of exile, the unification of the nation, the forgiving of the serious sins of the citizens, the making of an everlasting covenant of peace, the dwelling of God in their midst, and making Israel holy. Today's excerpt from Ezekiel is a prediction of the renewed vitality of the whole people after their exile from Jerusalem starting in 587 B.C. The people seemed dead: the Temple had been destroyed, the land wasted, and the leaders taken into custody.

Ezekiel puts forth the age-old hope of God: "I will be their God and they shall be my people" (v. 27). This technical covenant formula is comparable to the marriage formula, "I take you as my spouse." These were the "chosen people," a term applied to the physical descendants of Abraham whom God freely chose from among peoples in virtue of a promise He made to Abraham (Gn 17:2ff.).

The idea of the Jewish people as the special elect of God is often mentioned by the Jewish Scriptures. It was especially expressed in such passages as: "For you are a people sacred to the Lord, your God, who has chosen you from all the nations on the face of the earth to be a people peculiarly his own" (Dt 7:6; 14:2). G.K. Chesterton commented: "How odd of God to choose the Jews."

Widely different interpretations of this and similar passages range from claims that Jews have superior moral qualities to an objection that being chosen isn't a question of privilege at all. It rather implies greater spiritual responsibilities to be an example of the purest piety and humanity to all the rest of the world, and a need to develop a spiritual vitality worthy of those to whom God has chosen to transmit His revelation. Unfortunately, as the prophets and history remind us, the ancient Jews often fell into barbarity, wickedness, baseness of character, corruptness, and cruelty. The prophet Amos, among others, had to remind his people (3:2): "You alone have I favored, more than all the families of the earth; therefore I will punish you for all your crimes."

At present, Reform Jews de-emphasize the notion of a chosen people; they concentrate on the positive aspects of Diaspora Jewry and have deleted from their prayer book all references to a holy people. Reconstructionist Jewry advocates dropping the concept of chosenness for two reasons. One is to undercut accusations like those by George Bernard Shaw that if the Nazis had realized how Jewish their notion of Aryan supremacy was, they would have dropped it immediately — thus that the "chosen people" idea could be a model for racist ideologies. Secondly, the notion of chosenness should be dropped because it goes against modern thinking.

Throughout the lives of many, especially in the work-a-day world, people are confronted with conditions of chosenness. Why did one person get the position, the raise, the perks of position, and get to be looked upon as the so-called "elite"? What did he/she do to really deserve it? Why was he/she singled out for this privileged position?

St. Peter, applying to Christians a reference in the Jewish Scriptures to ancient Israel as "a kingdom of priests, a holy nation" (Ex 19:6), implies that those who believe in Jesus are the new chosen: "a chosen race, a royal priesthood, a holy nation, a people he claims for his own" (1 P 2:9). Yet the same Peter, speaking to the Gentile Cornelius, said "God shows no partiality" (Ac 10:34). St. Paul, the Apostle to the Gentiles, wrote to the Romans that "with God there is no favoritism" (Rm 2:11). To the Ephesians, Paul wrote of a "Master in heaven who plays no favorites" (Eph 6:9). Since Vatican Council II the preferred title for those who believe in Jesus is "the People of God." We belong to our God. But what sort of God? We must continually re-examine the image.

David stands out as one of the great shepherds, ruling over a united kingdom; and from him would come Jesus, the Good Shepherd. In the days of David and his son Solomon, the northern kingdom of Israel and the southern kingdom of Judah, later bitterly separated, were united. In Jesus the Holy Spirit would gather the children of God into the Church. "The character of universality which adorns the People of God is a gift from the

Lord himself whereby the Catholic Church ceaselessly and efficaciously seeks for the return of all humanity and all its goods, under Christ the Head in the unity of his Spirit" (Vatican II, *Lumen Gentium*, 13:2).

As for Jesus, the plan against him was self-serving and savage. The plot to kill him was the start of the wheels of injustice. Today's gospel reading shows, on the one hand, that many people who had witnessed Jesus' raising Lazarus from the dead and visited Lazarus's sister Mary came to an explosion of faith in Jesus (v. 45) that would continue through his triumphal entry into Jerusalem. Yet, because of Jesus' raising of Lazarus, many enemies were more determined than ever to kill him; some of them went to the Pharisees and told them the things that Jesus had done (v. 46). But the Pharisees wouldn't dare undertake anything without the consent of the chief priests. The authorities in Jerusalem would continue to monitor all Jesus' activities.

Jesus' enemies found a justification in the word of the chief priests that in order to save the people from the occupation of Jerusalem by Roman troops it was better that he die (vv. 46-48). The reasoning was that Jesus' popularity might result in an armed revolt against Rome in which blood might be spilled. By Jesus' death the people would be saved. The question of the high priest Caiaphas was like the one at the French Revolution: "Which is the more important: the nation or the king?"

In condemning Jesus to die in order to save the nation, Caiaphas spoke in prophecy without knowing it. He prophesied in the true sense — that is, he delivered a message from God. This gift doesn't necessarily imply holiness in its possessor, nor does it contain a claim that the prophet understands the full import of his words. His message was, indeed, full of irony: Jesus' death wouldn't prevent the Romans from coming and destroying the Temple and the city.

From then on, the consuming idea of Jesus' enemies was the illegal plan to put him to death (v. 53). Jesus, perhaps warned of their threatening intent by some of the highly connected kins-men of James and John, the sons of Zebedee, fled for the present to Ephraim, a town about twelve miles northeast of Jerusalem in the mountains descending into the Jordan valley, a day's jour-ney from the city. We can imagine the burden of the threat on Jesus, especially on feasts like the Passover that shortly followed (v. 55).

For Christians today, Sunday — our Sabbath — is a cel-ebration of the living presence of the risen Lord in the midst of the people of God. For this presence to be properly proclaimed and lived, it isn't enough that we pray to commemorate the death and resurrection of Christ in the secrecy of our individual hearts. It's important that we come *together* as the people of God to cel-ebrate life and express fully the very identity of the Church, the *ekklesia*, the assembly called together by the risen Lord who of-fered his life to reunite God's scattered children (v. 52). The Sunday celebration of the Lord's Day and his Eucharist is at the heart of the Church's life (*Catechism of the Catholic Church*, #41).

Monday of Holy Week
Is 42:1-7; Jn 12:1-11

Gentleness

Eight hundred New York City police officers took a special three-week course in kindness. In the course, they learned how to phrase questions and orders tactfully to avoid antagonizing people. They were told, for example, that an imperious-sounding question such as "What's your problem?" makes the person addressed feel defensive. Instead, the officers were advised to phrase the question in a positive, friendly way, like "Is something wrong? How can I help?" That phrasing conveys the message that the officer respects the other person and really wants to help.

When we treat other people with respect and consideration, they're likely to respond in the same way. Kindness brings out the best in us. Kindness is difficult to give away because it keeps coming back.

Today's Scripture readings combine an apostolic concern for world salvation, announced in Isaiah by the Lord's Suffering Servant as a light to the nations, with a gentle personal devotion to Jesus, shown in Mary of Bethany's silent anointing of Jesus' feet. Both are suffused with gentleness; no language is as universal and persuasive as that.

Isaiah catches the silence of Holy Week — gloomy, hopeful, strong. Each of Isaiah's four Suffering Servant songs gives a different insight into the soul of a mysterious Suffering Servant of God. Some have said the Servant is the Jewish people; Christian tradition sees these poems as referring to Jesus.

Today's first reading is the first of Isaiah's Servant songs which give a powerful and moving image of Jesus in his passion.

The words "I, the Lord, have called you to serve the cause of right, I have taken you by the hand and formed you," are addressed to every one of us. Holy Week shouldn't be simply a matter of devotion, but of seeing ourselves in the light of the passion of Jesus. We should be ready to take up our cross if and when that's called for.

Isaiah's very words came from heaven at Jesus' baptism, when the voice of the heavenly Father was almost verbatim the first line of Isaiah: The gospel expression "beloved son" means the same as Isaiah's "chosen one" of whom the Father approved. In Isaiah, the heavenly Father says that upon this servant He had put His Spirit (v. 1). This and the three other "Servant-of-the-Lord" oracles in Isaiah (49:1-7; 50:4-11; and 52:13-53:12) portray the ideal Servant of God, the perfect Israelite.

In this passage Isaiah is not, like in his other hymns, expansive, lyrical, and exultant: he's quiet to the point of being terse and melancholy. In the midst of traditional Jewish wisdom that God inflicted suffering only on those who deserved it, the idea that the holy and just might suffer innocently for others, was not only entirely new, it was revolutionary.

The way by which Jesus would bring God's message to the world would not be that of the triumphant military might of conquerors like Cyrus the Great, the Persian monarch in Isaiah's time who was on the march toward world empire. (Jesus' way contrasts, too, with some of our ways of dealing with others, sometimes even in our own family, parish, or neighborhood.) It would be the way of sacrificial love. The Servant accomplishes his mission quietly, gently, transforming from within (vv. 2-3). And pagan coast lands (v. 4) shall, like exiled Israel, experience an energetic striving for spiritual life and undergo a painful period of expectancy before the new life.

In addition to telling us that Jesus is the Suffering Servant of the Lord, this passage (plus other Scripture readings) tells us more about who Jesus is. He's the Anointed of the Lord or Mes-

siah (Christ), the Son of God, the Lord of all, the Healer of the
world, the Prophet who's to come into the world, the One who
ushers in the end of the ages. He's also the Lamb of God, Leader
of Life, Firstborn of the Dead, Head of His Body the Church, and
King of the Universe. None of those names exhaust the titles of
Jesus.

Also well chosen for the Monday of Holy Week is the account of Mary of Bethany's anointing the feet of Jesus. Hers was
a deed that showed how deeply she loved Jesus and how much
she wanted her giving to be a singular offering. The rawness of
her affection perhaps made those present uncomfortable: lavish,
gratuitous, affectionate, gift.

Jesus countered the audience's disapproval by completely
affirming what the woman had done and telling his uneasy, ob-
jecting hosts: "Leave her alone! She has done a good thing. The
poor you will always have with you.... She has just anointed me
for my impending death." Jesus could be stern with the proud,
and tender, gentle, and protective toward the humble and repentant.

The reaction of Judas Iscariot (v. 4) showed that he didn't
become a traitor overnight. Hiding his inward feelings, he seemed
to be saying to himself that it was useless to count any further
on Jesus; Jesus was lost, and the only thing for Judas to do was
to get what benefit he could from the situation. Stirred to resentment by the rebuke he received, the idea of betraying his master
entered his mind.

The contrast between Judas and Mary of Bethany is powerful. Mary spent what she had on "very costly ointment" in a gesture of love, affection, and respect. Judas complained that the
money for the ointment should have been given to the poor —
not really, but because he was a thief!

Jesus' comment (v. 7) was that the ointment was for the day
of his burial. The ancients considered proper anointing of the body
to be of great importance for a decent burial. Because there would

be no time to wash and anoint Jesus' body when he would die, this anointing took on even greater importance. The incident reflects one of the rabbinical discussions of the time about which was the greatest act of mercy: almsgiving or burying the dead.

The next person on the chief priests' hit list to be killed was Lazarus (v. 11). Because of Jesus having raised him from death, many Jews were coming to believe in Jesus. The killing of the unwanted goes on: abortion kills an unwanted child, euthanasia an unwanted elder, capital punishment an unwanted criminal. None of the perpetrators seems willing to admit the dignity of the individual human being. In Jesus' case, it never occurred to them that he was the embodiment of Isaiah's Servant of God.

Through it all, Jesus was gentle. As a distinctively Christian attribute, gentleness makes its first appearance in the second Beatitude: "Blessed are the gentle, for they shall inherit the earth." In an older (Douai) version of the Bible, the second Beatitude appears as "Blessed are the meek." The core notion has additional overtones of kindliness, courtesy, and mercy. Neither "gentle" nor "meek," however, means "submissive." In St. Paul's Letter to the Galatians, gentleness is listed among the fruits of the Holy Spirit: "Love, joy, peace, patience, kindness, goodness, trustfulness, gentleness, and self-control."

St. Thomas Aquinas saw both gentleness and mercy as subsidiary expressions of love, the greatest of all the virtues, and as promoting the love of one's neighbor in the same way as compassion and respectful duty do. Both gentleness and mercy are contrasted, in St. Thomas's account, with anger, which "because of its force especially prevents the mind from freely judging the truth." Gentleness in particular, he thought, "prepares us for the knowledge of God" by giving us self-control.

Christian gentleness doesn't preclude anger in a just cause, but restrains and modifies it. Notions of compassion, forgiveness, generosity, attention to truth, and above all kindness are included in it: Indeed, each "fruit of the Spirit" partakes to some degree of all the others, although each has its own emphasis. Gentleness is a facet of holiness and, as such, a product of prayer.

In large organizations, whether in the public or private sector, the proliferation of bureaucratic controls, insistence on greater professionalism, and the relentless drive to maximize profits are leaving less and less room for gentleness. If today's threat to gentleness is less direct than in the past, it's no less insidious. And the prevalence of violence on film and television, and the drive to push out the barriers of what is publicly acceptable in terms of brutality, are anesthetizing us to ugliness of conduct in ways which would have been impossible before the arrival of the electronic media.

Evidence of the threat to gentleness comes not only from a reluctance to forgive, but from the heightened readiness on all sides to criticize rather than to excuse. A glance at the correspondence columns of even the Catholic press shows anger and resentment as a common currency of debate. It's hard to avoid the feeling that letters are often written and comments made more with the intention of hurting those with whom one disagrees than with any desire to understand or tolerate opposing points of view. But a world of justice without kindness is repugnant to the Christian spirit.

It's evident that neither Christians individually nor the Church collectively always behave gently. But uncovenanted generosity, forgiveness, and understanding of human frailty have always been at the heart of what Christ's followers are about. In today's brave new secularized world, a great contribution which Christians can make toward keeping the faith alive is to ensure the survival of gentleness.

The Suffering Servant reflects life experience by way of gentleness; Judas, by betrayal. We're all capable of going either way. God loves everyone, but prefers "fruits of the Spirit" over "religious nuts"!

Handling Betrayal: Judas and Peter

Today's gospel presents two people who are important to Holy Week: Judas and St. Peter. Both of them, like all of us whom Jesus has called, are flawed: combinations of strengths and weaknesses. Judas is abhorrent to us, Peter attractive.

Last Sunday — Passion or Palm Sunday — Judas saw Jesus' exciting entrance to Jerusalem as an occasion to emphasize the triumphalistic character of the kingdom. When Jesus didn't capitalize on the triumph of that day, Judas and others like him lost enthusiasm. Judas's betrayal of Jesus may have contained a good measure of self-justifying rationalization that may have gone something like this.

"Sure I helped stir up the crowds, their fever-pitched 'Hosannas' rocking the walls of Jerusalem. I wanted him to only say the word, and we'd roust the Romans out of here. Instead he reminded me to love my enemies and forgive. Time was running out; I had to act. I believed *too much*. I had seen his power. I was convinced that once he felt the sword at his throat he would invoke the power of God and destroy the infidels! But I was wrong. He submitted without a word. And I, who sought to force his hand, couldn't bear to see him taken like a common criminal. From this day on all generations will call me traitor, because I couldn't believe that God's power to save exceeded my power to sin. Unworthy of forgiveness, I envy all who are strong enough to wait. For me there's now only one way out: to hang myself."

Beyond the possible thinking of Judas, the existence of evil has engendered perennial questioning. The mystery of evil — and that is what it is, mystery, not a problem to be solved — raises for Christian thinkers a challenge unlike any other, for it suggests that the existence of evil is incompatible with the existence of God. How is it possible to affirm, without contradiction, that God is all-powerful and all good, and at the same time evil exists?

The mystery deepens when evil is made to encompass such diverse phenomena as cancer, earthquake, and "nature red in tooth and claw," which are evil on a grand scale exceeding all imaginable compensation. What tells most against all explanations is the grossly disproportionate and wholly senseless evil of human-caused tragedies such as Auschwitz, Rwanda, and the World Trade Center, evils whose dimension can't be charted or absorbed. Beyond all the discussion are the silent, burning tears of those who suffer and ask, "Why this evil to me?"

There's a dialectic moving from Adam to Job to Jesus; from suffering as penalty to suffering as affliction; from culprit to victim to servant; from evil committed to evil suffered to evil redeemed; from God as lawgiver/judge to God as tyrant to God as fellow-sufferer and advocate. Always there are the tears of children, mass deaths, and the nightmare of the cruel or ineffective God of tragedy.

Always captivating has been the primal act of betrayal. Dante reserved the Ninth Circle of Hell, its bottom, for betrayers: Judas, the betrayer of Jesus, and Brutus and Cassius, the betrayers of Julius Caesar. Dante froze betrayers in ice, because they were breaking faith with friends; through their betrayal they had ceased to have the capacity for love and so for heaven.

How much more attractive than Judas is Peter. A charismatic leader, Peter was nevertheless aware that he had often left much to be desired. Called impetuous, a less benevolent interpreter might call him thoughtless. Jesus had alternately called him "the Rock" and "Satan." Jesus took him, along with John and his brother James, to the mountain of the transfiguration, hoping that their memory of that glorious event might serve to safeguard against the surprise of his agony. Selfishly, Peter wanted that glory to continue forever; he babbled about building three tents so they could stay there: one for Jesus, one for Moses, and one for Elijah. He was willing to forget their other duties and even the other nine Apostles.

When Jesus had given him permission to walk on water, and then Peter saw the first difficulty coming his way in the form of a wave, his faith began to leave and he began to sink. And there were other times: when he'd stupidly chided Jesus at the Lord's prediction of his passion, when he'd childishly wanted to know how many times to forgive injuries, when at the Last Supper he didn't want Jesus to wash his feet, when in the garden of Gethsemane he'd slept and then impulsively cut off the ear of the High Priest's servant. Shame overshadowed the Last Supper when Peter was so overconfident that he told Jesus he was prepared to die with him; Jesus foretold his threefold denials before the crowing of the roosters early the next morning, and so it came to pass.

There's a word in today's gospel that seems out of place: that upon Judas' betrayal Jesus and God are "glorified" (v. 31f.). In the context of Jesus' imminent arrest, condemnation, and crucifixion, where's the glory? Yet this word is the key to understanding it all. In John's gospel, the passion of Jesus is the climax of his entire mission of mercy, love, forgiveness, and healing, as well as his awesome victory over sin and death. Jesus says, "I am not to be with you much longer" — he's going for glory. He adds, "Later on you shall come after me": we're going for glory, too.

Like the second song of the Servant of Yahweh in today's first reading, sometimes we think that all our labor is in vain and that we've exhausted ourselves for nothing. When that happens we must remember that God called us before we were born, and called us by name from our mother's womb. Peter didn't believe Jesus' prediction of his treachery because Peter didn't know himself. Deep down in everyone there's a potential for both good and evil. We don't want to face the possibility of evil. And we must always remember that grace is more powerful than sin.

Even Judas had many God-given opportunities of coming to his senses. Jesus didn't deny him his companionship. He didn't take away the dignity of his Apostleship. He didn't even take the purse strings away, even though Judas was a thief. Jesus admitted the traitor to the fellowship of his disciples at the Last Supper. He deigned to stoop to the feet of the betrayer to wash his feet. With incomparable generosity he gave him his bread to eat — that body which he had already sold — and his blood to drink — that blood which he had already set flowing. Even when Judas came with his crew to seize him and kissed him — that kiss which was a remembrance of his treachery — Jesus received him calmly and gently. Since Jesus showed his great mercy in so many ways even toward Judas, there's no reason why, in this life, anyone should despair.

Peter was guilty of denial that was tantamount to betrayal, and Judas of actual betrayal. The difference between them? Peter had an attitude of trust and therefore surrender; ultimately, he gladly gave his life for Jesus. Judas, on the other hand, had an attitude of selfish distrust and therefore fled from Jesus; this resulted in his hanging himself in despair.

We've all been guilty of denying or betraying Jesus in one way or another. When we recognize that, let's imitate the humility and hopefulness of Peter rather than the despair of Judas, and make ourselves right with the Lord.

Against Pride: Submission to God's Will

Someone recently opined about what he would do if he were the devil. He thought like this.

"I'd gain control of the most powerful nation in the world. I'd delude its peoples' minds into thinking that their virtues had come from their own unassisted efforts instead of God's blessings. I'd promote an attitude of loving things and using people, instead of the other way around. I'd convince people that leadership has nothing to do with character. I'd make it legal to take the life of unborn people. I'd make it socially acceptable to take one's own life, and invent pills and machines to make that convenient. I'd cheapen human life as much as possible so that the lives of animals would be valued at least as much as human beings.

"I'd take God out of the schools, where even the mention of His name would be grounds for a lawsuit. I'd come up with drugs that sedate the mind and target the young, and I'd get sports heroes to advertise them. I'd get control of the media, so that every night I could tune the mind of every family member to my agenda.

"I'd attack the family, the backbone of a nation. I'd make divorce fashionable. I'd make it possible for people to express their most depraved fantasies on canvas and movie screens, and I'd call it art. I'd convince people that right and wrong are determined by a few who call themselves authorities and are 'out of it.' I'd persuade people that the Church is irrelevant and out of date, and the Bible is for the naive. I'd dull the minds of Christians, and make them believe that prayer isn't important and that faithfulness and obedience are optional.

"On second thought," the man concluded, "I guess I'd leave things pretty much the way they are."

Today's first reading, from the third of Isaiah's four Suffering Servant songs, is an uncannily exact description of Jesus in his passion — his suffering for all the sins of the human race. This Servant of God is the personification of the one who exemplified the best goals and traits of the people of God: to overcome evil by good, violence by love, war by peace-making. In today's song, at the degradation meted out to him, the Suffering Servant showed exceptional strength. As he winced from the strikes on his back, stared through the tears engulfing his eyes, and recoiled from the spittle flung grossly upon his cheeks, he surrendered in spirit to God. Nothing would rob him of his interior peace and dignity.

Jesus, the ideal Israelite, was docile before the Father, but determined, firm, and silent in the face of suffering. For him to go along with the people's notion of a wonder-working and powerful Messiah, and to try to *be* that kind of Messiah, was another opportunity for the Tempter!

Yet more than Suffering Servant, Jesus is God, Master and Owner of all life. The heavenly Father's voice had called him His Son at his baptism and again at his transfiguration, angels and demons had called him the Son of God, the challenging High Priest had taken Jesus' affirmation of his godhood seriously enough to call it blasphemy, and the centurion would confess to his divinity at his death. This Suffering Servant of God should receive cosmic adoration as an act of religious devotion.

Why, then, did he receive instead the shabby betrayal of a Judas? In today's gospel, part of St. Matthew's account of the Last Supper, we see the treachery of Judas even more than in the portion of St. John's account that we read yesterday. The traitor asks Jesus, along with the others, whether the betrayer was he. To admit one's sin and to turn to God in sorrow is the only way to deal with it. Judas had that chance, but missed it. Even at the table of the Paschal Meal, the shame of betrayal overshadowed him. The Eucharist is no complete guarantee against the possibility of violation of trust.

Betrayal is one of the worst — and possibly even the most destructive — crimes to commit or experience. It tears us apart at the core of our existence — that core where we establish and maintain our relationships of trust, love, and security. *Every* sin does that; *every* evil raises barriers between us and others. Explicit betrayal, though, cuts the deepest of all and inflicts the worst scars. This kind of injury often incapacitates everyone for happy living. Those who betray tend to isolate themselves; those who are betrayed feel violated.

All who are betrayed suffer greatly. Lonely, they're unable to set up the normal contacts required for simple conversations. The betrayal has struck most profoundly at the heart of their existence, rubbing raw the deepest levels of love and affection. In the case of the Son of God, even though he knew that Judas was seeking his chance to betray him, Jesus with majesty invited Judas along with the other Apostles to share his Last Supper. Jesus tried desperately to salvage Judas from his despicable act. It didn't work.

How is it possible to betray? In Judas's case, based upon the scriptural record of his being a thief, one of his weaknesses was avarice. Another was pride — thinking that he had a better way than Jesus. And his pride was looking forward to a high place of influence in a coming kingdom.

Traditionally pride was considered the most deadly of the deadly sins, the source of all sin. Once upon a time Lucifer, the great angel of light, fell from heaven, banished from bliss forever because, in his overweening pride, he challenged the Almighty. No one thinks Eve bit the apple because she was greedy, lazy, angry, envious, lustful, or covetous. She ate it because she was too proud to be submissive to God and, like Adam, wanted to be, not God-like, but like God. All other sins stem from that —

ᴜ believing that we can go it on our own, that we know ᴇr, that we don't need anyone, that we can make up our own ᴍind by ourselves.

Today, pride is considered a virtue. To accept anyone or anything as superior is thought to be cowardice at best, and psychopathic at worst. The approved characteristics today are independence, self-sufficiency, autonomy, originality, creativity, self-expression, and self-esteem. Low self-esteem is thought to be the cause of most personal woes; reducing the self-esteem of another is debasing rather than educational; assertiveness is desirable. People with low self-esteem were (unintentionally and humorously) denigrated even by the parish church sign that read: "Low Self-Esteem Support Group will meet Thursday. Please use the back door."

The thinking of such wrong-headed people says that shame is wrong, guilt is neurotic. They've changed the language, too: The virtue of humility is now the sin of self-hatred, the sin of selfishness has now become the virtue of being fulfilled, discourtesy is now termed frankness, and disobedience is now called freedom.

Inevitably, pride is a *virtue* in a society based on the rights of the individual. Equally, pride is a *sin* for believers in God, for precisely the same reason — because it strengthens the boundaries of individuals and makes them less permeable to the intrusion of the Other.

This week is a good time to learn the depth of betrayal of which we're all capable — and act upon it. An old story tells of Pastor Niemoeller, who was a victim of the Holocaust in Germany. He reasoned for his inaction: "When the Nazis came for the Communists, I was silent: I wasn't a Communist. When the Nazis came for the Social Democrats, I was silent: I wasn't a Social Democrat. When the Nazis came for the Trade Unionists, I was silent: I wasn't a Trade Unionist. When the Nazis came for the Jews, I was silent: I wasn't a Jew. When the Nazis came for me, there was no one left to protest."

One reason for the changes in our time is that we've become the victims of a phenomenon which probably comes between many people and God: religious indifference. Although the word is little used, there are probably more adiaphorists (people who are religiously indifferent) than theists, deists, agnostics, and atheists put together. Sad to say, moral relativism has meant that large numbers of people have become adiaphorists in matters of public ethics as well.

Despite whatever our self-examination reveals of our particular weaknesses, we have a way back through the sacrament of Reconciliation. With that gift, we're assured that nothing outside of us can ever rob us of our interior peace and dignity, unless we let it.

oly Thursday

Ex 12:1-8,11-14; 1 Cor 11:23-26; Jn 13:1-15

Mass of the Lord's Supper, Evening

St. John the beloved disciple recorded here that at their last meal together, on this night before Jesus was to die, he loved all his followers completely — that is, to death, the limit of love's perfection. Our first reading, from the Book of Exodus, gives the regulations for the Passover supper. Today's gospel took place when the Lord's Passover supper had hardly begun, and when it was still the proper time for ablutions. To wash the feet of another was considered at that time so lowly that it couldn't be demanded even of a slave. Jesus reached the heights of heroism when, even knowing of the betrayal, he washed Judas's feet. And the one who protested the washing of the feet wasn't Judas, but Peter! Peter was still impulsive, but had by now grown into a degree of humility. Judas said nothing.

With the cup of wine that was appointed to be drunk last, in thanksgiving for the Paschal supper, Jesus did something unusual. He changed bread and wine into his body and blood. He first blessed the bread and wine, giving thanks to his heavenly Father for His gifts and calling the divine blessing upon this food and drink. Jesus' prayer is substantially repeated in the Mass. His words, "this is my body" and "this is my blood," are not only *declarative*, but *operative*, and have been so understood from the earliest days of Christianity. Jesus' telling us that his body and blood "shall be given up for you" alludes to the sacrificial lambs, and has a character of making amends.

Jesus' Eucharistic supper doesn't differ *substantially* from the sacrifice of the cross. What differs is the mode of sacrifice. In the Eucharistic supper the separation of the flesh and the blood is mystical; it's nevertheless a true sacrifice, and may be spoken of as the first Mass. Nor does the Mass differ *substantially* from the sacrifice of the cross; it differs as to the method of offering. Whereas the sacrificial banquet at the Last Supper is in *anticipation* of Calvary, all repetitions of the liturgy of the Last Supper by the Church are *memorial* sacrifices.

It's that memorial which St. Paul was talking about in his First Letter to the Corinthians, the earliest written account of the institution of the Eucharist. Paul presents a profound theology of that meal. He uses the Greek word *anamnesis*, which we translate as *remembrance*, or *memory* (v. 24). This in turn translates the Hebrew *ziccaron,* a First Testament word which means *memorial sacrifice.*

Jesus' request at the Last Supper, that we do this in memory of him, is among the most poignant of his statements in the entire New Testament. It's difficult to interpret his command, which we repeat at the Eucharistic celebration right after the consecration: "Do this in memory of me." Surely we don't emphasize the prepositions. But if we say, "*Do* this...," we're emphasizing the action. If we say, "Do *this*...," we're emphasizing the Last Supper. If we say, "Do this in *memory*...," we're emphasizing the present and future as well as the past. And if we say, "Do this in memory of *me*," we're putting our emphasis on Jesus and his suffering. All these emphases are valid.

What Jesus meant by *this* is what he himself did: to bless and thank God for his life, death, and resurrection, and to celebrate it in the Eucharist. *This* is a simple thing that's gone on throughout Christian history and is to last forever. Christians have found nothing better than *this* to do for condemned Christians as the lions roared in the nearby amphitheater; for kings at their crowning and for criminals going to the scaffold; for armies in triumph and for wedding couples in little country churches; for a sick elderly woman about to die and for Columbus setting sail; for an exiled bishop who had hewn timber all day in a prison camp and for an old monk on the fiftieth anniversary of his vows. The Eucharist has been celebrated in every conceivable human circumstance and for every conceivable human need, in every century since Jesus, on every continent, and among every race on earth.

It's as though Jesus said, "Remember me, and all that I've said and done in your presence. Remember my love. If at first some people don't understand, have them remember the yearnings of all people's hearts and the need to express their love. And I hope all of you will remember that *I* love *you* so much that I'm giving all I have, my very blood, for you."

In his First Letter to the Corinthians, Paul is trying to show that the celebration of the Eucharist is a memorial sacrifice by which God remembers to shower mercy upon us because of the death of His Son. Through the Eucharist, Christians of all times have found themselves again with their Savior in making present Jesus' great redeeming sacrifice. We've so often heard the words of the Eucharist at every Mass that we can easily take them for granted. Imagine the amazement, if not the incredulity, of the Apostles when they heard them for the first time!

So the Eucharist is not only to be a memory, but a living contact with Jesus. As Paul wrote to the Corinthians, one can't at the same time be self-centered and *truly* celebrate the Eucharist. This sacrifice is functional: It's *for you.* Paul understands the egalitarian aspect of Jesus' activity, and addresses the question of social divisions in the group with regard to eating together. The rich Christians who had plenty of leisure came early and ate the best food, not waiting for the arrival of their fellow Christians who were slaves. This *new* covenant is the fulfillment of God's promises to Jeremiah (31:31) to replace God's Mosaic covenant.

The Eucharist, the most exalted of all the Sacraments, is essentially a meal, like the one that Jesus shared with the people in the meadow when he multiplied the bread and fish. It intends to bring together not only us with God, but us with one another. St. Thomas Aquinas spoke in terms of the ultimate change in the Eucharist being not only the transubstantiation of the bread and wine into Jesus' body and blood, but the transformation of ourselves into Jesus' presence. Our communion means that we *receive* the body of Christ in the Eucharist and *perceive* the body of Christ in our neighbor. We can't share fruitfully in the former if we're unmindful of the latter.

When as a family we have a meal at home together, we're drawn closer by that sharing. When we provide hospitality to friends by way of a meal — or they for us — we have the opportunity for closeness with one another that nothing else has. In the Eucharist, God is providing the same opportunity, with the addition that it's God and His unique abundance that provide the closeness, intimacy, union, and other rewards.

If we want the Eucharist to contribute to our spiritual nourishment, as Jesus intended, we must approach it with *reverence*. That means profound respect. Reverence includes many other things: love, awe, affection, tenderness, honor, self-abnegation, veneration, worship, and adoration.

Reverence differs from and is above all of those things. It's different from mere *honor*, which is recognition through giving great respect to high and deserving personages; or *homage*, which is the idea of praise or tribute, especially from one owing allegiance, as to a bishop; or *deference*, which implies a yielding or submitting to the judgment of a learned person; or *obeisance*, which implies a show of honor by self-humbling gestures like bowing or kneeling.

How are we to reverence the Eucharist? Spiritually, we approach with as much purity as we can muster. Bodily, reverence for the Eucharist means cleanliness, proper dress, punctuality, a realization of the importance of what we do, and courtesy. We believe in the importance of the body because, for one thing, the eternal Word of God took human flesh in the person of Jesus of

Nazareth. We celebrate his body, which he identified with bread and wine at his Last Supper, given us as the food of faith

The Eucharist, Jesus' continued presence in the community of faith, is Christianity's most precious possession; all aspects of this breathtaking reality require profound purity of body and soul. And the realization that we all — rich and poor, similar and dissimilar — receive the same Lord should increase our awareness that we're one human family.

In the last sentence of today's reading from his First Letter to the Corinthians, Paul uses the word *proclaim* — that every time we eat this bread and drink this cup, we *proclaim* the death of the Lord until he comes. The word that Paul uses (*katangellete*) means "to celebrate in a living way, to bring to the present and make effective here and now." In other words, when we proclaim the death of the Lord until he comes, we're bringing Christ to the present and making him effective in ourselves. Without the Eucharist, there can be no sufficient satisfaction for our hunger for peace, or justice, or love.

Good Friday
Is 52:13-53:12; Heb 4:14-16; 5:7-9; Jn 18:1-19:42

What Jesus Saw from the Cross

The mound of Calvary was the place called the Skull, in Hebrew Golgotha (probably a small hill resembling a skull). It rose about sixteen feet above the surrounding area. Jesus' cross was about ten feet high; it was considered sufficient if the victim's feet just cleared the ground. Dogs and jackals drawn by the scent of blood sometimes devoured the feet, and vultures circled overhead. The cross was outside the west of the city, its highest point.

Mosaic Law recognized four forms of death for recalcitrant Jews: stoning, burning, beheading, and strangling. Stoning was the most usual. The victim was flung from a high place and, if still alive, stoned until dead. But it was Roman law under which Jesus was being put to death, by crucifixion. This was forbidden for a Roman citizen, and this shame and dishonor were for only the very lowest criminals — slaves, provincial malefactors, and the like.

Jesus had been roughly placed on the "seat," the *sedile*, or *cornu* (horn), a piece of wood projecting in the middle of the upright beam. This supported him while being nailed and after, and prevented the nails from ripping through his wrists. His arms were fastened to the horizontal beam that he had carried; this was then attached to the vertical beam which was staked on the site. His feet were nailed to the cross. The usual victim was left exposed to the sun, torn by pain, hunger, and thirst, until his executioners, weary of his agony, dispatched him with the breaking of his legs.

Here outside the Gate of Ephraim, or "Gate of the Square," Jesus faced east, toward the gate and the city. Northeast, slightly to his left in the distance, he could see Mount Scopus, where the young Greek conqueror Alexander had once quailed before the majesty of the high priest, and where the Roman general Titus would encamp when, about thirty-seven years hence, he would doom the city of Jerusalem to utter destruction.

Through the city gates, Jesus saw the continuous stream of people flowing between two animated banks of itinerant merchants, wheeled stalls along with permanent booths all along the street selling drinks and sweetmeats. Beggars, especially the blind (numerous because of infections caused by the heat and the dirt in the air), cripples, paralytics, and lepers more or less healed, were raising their cries. That was the street Jesus had been forced to take to Calvary.

Jesus saw an oriental city on the eve of a festival (this time

Passover), with people arriving by the tens of thousands, everyone in a great hurry. Hawkers were assuring for themselves
months of frugal life in a short time: water in goatskin gourds,
sweetmeats favored by visiting villagers, fresh and dried fruits
and sugared almonds, lemonade in tanks. Also, purveyors of
goats, sheep, doves, and cattle for the sacrifices were driving their
herds toward the Temple enclosure. On the way to Calvary, Jesus
hadn't been able to see the steps in the street for the crowds, and
had fallen several times. Some in the crowd were friends, secret
or avowed; some, perhaps many, were sympathizers; and there
were the indifferent, the inquisitive, the scoffers, and enemies,
official or otherwise.

About half a mile across the city, Jesus could see the garden of Gethsemane. It was there that he and his close followers
had spent nights when there was no time to get as far as the home
of Martha, Mary, and Lazarus at Bethany. Last night, Jesus had
been in agony there over his fight or flight decision. Judas knew
the place; he also knew that Jesus had slipped from the hands of
his enemies before (Lk 4:29f.; Jn 8:59; 12:3, 6). Judas had seen
to it that that didn't happen this time.

Beyond Gethsemane and the Mount of Olives were the
Mountains of Moab. There was Mt. Nebo, whence Moses saw the
Promised Land and made his touching dying speech to his people.
Somewhere in those hills was also the Fortress Machaerus, where
Herod Antipas had had John the Baptist beheaded. Jericho, eight
miles closer, near the Jordan River, provided Jesus with memo-
ries of his baptism and his heavenly Father's voice from heaven.
Nearer was the Golden Gate, through which he had jubilantly
entered the city on Palm Sunday less than a week ago.

To the south — over his right shoulder — Jesus could see
the Cenacle, where last night he had taught his people so many
things on the eve of his death and gave them the Eucharist to
sustain them through the hard times ahead.

Less than a quarter mile away in front of him he could see

the Temple — in its magnificence now, with the afternoon sun behind him shining fully on it. It was to that sacred place, to which his parents had brought him in his youth and where he had gone to celebrate many festivals and where he had taught, that he had been led before the high priest Annas. From his questioning of Jesus, Annas had seen at once that his purposes weren't to be gained as easily as he had expected. Once his curiosity had been satisfied, he refused to take any responsibility; he had learned discretion. During Annas' interrogation, a surly attendant had struck Jesus, who remained perfectly controlled.

Near the Temple area, he could also see the meeting place of the Sanhedrin. In this emergency, they had held a night session about him — grossly illegal, though the Sanhedrin always tried to act with a *semblance* of legality. The Romans allowed the Sanhedrin the right to condemn a man to death, but required that the sentence be ratified by the Roman procurator, currently Pontius Pilate.

Without so much as ordering the removal of the bonds from Jesus' hands, Annas had sent him across town to the house of the high priest Caiaphas, visible further to Jesus' right. To Caiaphas' house had come some of the influential members of the priesthood, along with doctors of the Mosaic Law and elders of the people, to conduct a preliminary examination of the prisoner. Jesus, who was always eager to preach the kingdom of God to men of good will, had nothing to say before this assembly.

Each crossing of the city meant traversing the Tyropean Valley, a filled-in depression which cut through the city from north to south, which meant further strain. To make matters worse, Jesus knew that Peter, who had protested his loyalty at the Last Supper, was denying being a follower of Jesus. After the third denial, a rooster crowed, as Jesus had predicted. That was about 2:30 a.m., the time when roosters usually began to crow. Through it all, Jesus had been continuously insulted and mocked. And Judas had hung himself.

Jesus saw the Fortress Antonia, the highest position in the upper city and overlooking the Temple. Pilate had taken up residence there so as to keep an eye on the doings of the pilgrims. As the palace of Herod, used for such occasions, was inhabited by pagans and used for the administration of their authority, for Jews it was ritually unclean in the highest degree. So Pilate held this hearing in the Praetorium, the place sometimes used for judgments. The soldiers meanwhile amused themselves by whipping this Jew Jesus who posed as a king. They scorned all kings and held the Jews in contempt.

Pilate, already fully informed about this trial by his police, appeared at a balcony of the palace. The leaders, with bluff and bluster, at first tried to have Pilate ratify their sentence of death without investigating the case. The case, in Pilate's mind, provided a cost-free reward to fling at the Temple administration. He despised these people.

The leaders opened by saying it wasn't lawful for them to put anyone to death. Death had not yet been mentioned; the leaders were showing their hand. Pilate opened by getting to the heart of the matter for Rome. He asked Jesus if he did, indeed, claim to be the king of the Jews, as his prosecutors were asserting. If true, this would be tantamount to rebellion. Because Pilate's mind connected kingship with splendor and power and that wasn't what Jesus stood for, Jesus had to answer in the negative.

The craftiness of the leaders in giving the matter a political complexion which was well-calculated to overexcite the irascible Pilate equaled their guile at other times — when, for example, they had asked Jesus about tribute money to Caesar. In order to learn what was the charge against him, Jesus asked whether Pilate was speaking on his own initiative or repeating something the Jews had alleged (v. 34).

Jesus asserted that his kingdom is not of this world. In terms that Pilate might understand, he added that if his kingdom were of this world, his followers would have fought — the best proof of the spiritual nature of his kingship. If Jesus had wanted to establish a kingdom, this Passover time with its crowds would have provided an ideal opportunity. Jesus had close followers and was extremely popular among the masses. Pilate knew all of that as well as Jesus did.

Jesus told Pilate that he came into the world to witness to *truth:* about God, about people, about life. He wouldn't kill for the truth; he would die for it. He would win, not by spilling the blood of others, but by offering his own. To Pilate's question — what is truth? — Pilate expected no answer because he thought none was possible. Pilate, a pragmatic administrator, professed contempt for speculation. Pilate ended the first part of the Roman trial by declaring Jesus innocent of the charge of sedition.

Then Pilate, hearing that Jesus belonged to the Galilean jurisdiction of Herod Antipas, and wanting to unload the case, sent Jesus to him. Antipas was delighted. For one thing, up to now Pilate and he had been enemies because of Pilate's high-handed treatment of the Galileans in Jerusalem (Lk 13:1f.). Also, Antipas wanted to question Jesus, about whom he'd heard so much. But because Antipas was so centered in himself that he wouldn't be able to hear any answers, Jesus gave none. He's the only recorded person with whom Jesus refused to speak. Antipas had him arrayed in a flashy robe and sent back to Pilate.

Pilate tried to appease the Jews by the halfway measure of having him severely whipped, sometimes a good means of persuading fanatics to hold their tongues. At the sight of the horribly stripped and beaten Jesus the soldiers, knowing that he had been accused of attempting to usurp royal dignity, recalled an ancient comedy of a shadow king. They made a crown from a bundle of thorns gathered for the fire, forced it down on his head and, bowing before him, made fun of him.

Pilate had then urged Jesus' accusers to look at the man. Pilate wasn't so naïve as to think that the Jews would feel compassion; he wanted them to see that there was nothing to be feared from a man in his condition. When that only fired up their leaders with more shouts for crucifixion, he had told them to take him themselves and crucify him. If they had dared to take his proposal seriously, Pilate would have gotten some satisfaction out of reporting them to Rome.

But the Jews had no intention of falling into that trap. Seeing that Pilate was unmoved by their charge of Jesus being a revolutionary agitator, they at last disclosed their real complaint against him. In matters concerning their religion, they alone were competent to judge right and wrong. They had a Law, they said, whereby anyone who was so blasphemous as to claim to be God must die. So perverted had the Law of God become in their hands that God's own Son must die by it!

Pilate had then made a last effort to save this innocent man. First, because he was superstitious, he asked Jesus where he was from — an inquiry about the world of the gods. When Jesus didn't answer, he reminded Jesus of his power to have him released or crucified. Jesus in turn reminded Pilate that he would have no power at all if it hadn't been given him from above. These were Jesus' last words to Pilate. Pilate was alarmed and desired to release this prisoner of so rare a character.

The Jews, aware of Pilate's dilemma, fired their last shot by threatening Pilate that if he released this man, they wouldn't consider him to be a friend of Caesar. Pilate was well aware that the Emperor Tiberius gave every encouragement to informers. Pilate's pragmatism told him that it would be fatal for him if the report reached Tiberius that he had caused a riot by opposing the Jews precisely in a matter where they appeared more anxious to preserve the Roman dominion in Palestine than he himself was.

He finally handed Jesus over to be crucified. He had been sucked into the depths of "the powers of darkness," into a confusion so dark and deep that he was no longer sensitive to the gruesome folly he was committing. History doesn't remember Pilate except in connection with this trial.

After their leaders' success, the bulk of the people went to attend to the chief work of that day, preparation for the Passover. Jesus' agony, however, continued. Some passersby, remembering Jesus' misunderstood prophecy about the destruction of the Temple, defied him to come down from the cross. Others shouted that Jesus had trusted in God, so God should deliver him now. One of the two thieves crucified at his side, in his ignorance and out of his habit of cursing, said the same kinds of things. The four soldiers, who had the duty of seeing to it that the victim died on the cross, divided his garments among themselves.

Through the betrayal, the injustice, the pain, the misunderstandings, the bare hatred, and the aloneness, Jesus spoke from his cross. He beseeched his heavenly Father to forgive his murderers, because they didn't know what they were doing. He promised the crucified thief who kept asking for pardon that he would soon get into heaven. He had been rejected by the leaders as a blasphemer, handed over to strangers, treated by the Romans as a criminal, spurned by the people, jeered at by a thief, and forsaken by his friends. There was only one more affliction for his soul to bear, but that was the cruelest: abandonment by his heavenly Father. From the bottom of his soul he cried for God's help.

One of his utterances received a response. He said that he was thirsty, and a soldier offered him the common wine which was the ordinary drink of the Roman soldiers. It was like vinegar. The soldier could only give what he had. Jesus couldn't drink it.

Looking down to the foot of his cross, Jesus saw his mother. Of all his followers, she was suffering the most. During the night, reports about events had one by one reached her. The next morning, she had heard the shouts calling for his death. She had met him on his way to Calvary. She saw how they had nailed him to the cross. She wished she could take his place. She was enduring what no parent should ever have to: the death of her child. In union with him she, too, experienced abandonment.

In a dying voice, heard only by the little group of his faithful friends in the midst of the continuing blasphemies, Jesus was putting his mother in the care of the young St. John, whose affection for her was full of respect and tenderness. John was given to her in place of himself, the disciple in place of the master, the son of Zebedee in place of her son, the Son of God. All of it went right through her loving heart!

By the time Jesus announced that it was all over, the sun would ordinarily be at its brightest; but darkness covered the place, the thirty-yard-high veil of the Temple was torn from top to bottom, the rock of Golgotha was split, and the crucified thief and the centurion, who were accustomed to scenes of blood, were converted. Jesus committed his soul to his heavenly Father and died. His suffering and death had intermingled two currents of events, one bearing on the then-and-there and the other sowing the seeds of eternal life forever in the universe of souls.

Today's readings from Isaiah and the Letter to the Hebrews put it into perspective. Isaiah presents the fourth and last of his passages on the Suffering Servant of Yahweh. It tells us that it's our infirmities that the man of suffering bore; upon him was the chastisement that makes us whole. He was like a lamb led to slaughter. His suffering would win pardon for the sins of many.

The Letter to the Hebrews gives a more detailed and glorious picture; few passages in the New Testament are so packed with meaning. It says that Jesus prayed, even with loud cries and tears (5:7) — the kind of cries and tears that are wrung from a person by searing pain. Through his suffering, Jesus learned and grew (v. 8) to the point of being able to accept suffering with reverence.

The passage offers the comforting image of the Son of God who drew near us, and invites us to draw near him. He showed his greatness not only as God, but also as a human being. Because he came among us and was tested in every way (4:15), he's able to sympathize with our weaknesses. Through what he did, the throne of God became the throne of grace (4:16).

Be Happy!

Tonight's service is in four parts. First is the service of light, which consists of the blessing of the fire, lighting of the candle, and the Easter proclamation (*Exultet*). The second, in which we are now participating, is the Liturgy of the Word, on all the wonderful things God has done for His people from the beginning. Still to come are the Liturgy of Baptism, when new members of the Church are reborn as the day of resurrection approaches. This contains a litany, blessing of the water, renunciation of sin, profession of faith, and the reception of new converts, if there are any. Fourth and last will be the Liturgy of the Eucharist, when the whole Church is called to the table which the Lord has prepared for his people through his death and resurrection.

All of our liturgy, and each of our Scripture readings, are full of meaning and joy. It behooves us to try to perceive the meaning of the three readings that are minimum for this celebration.

In today's passage from the Book of Exodus, Pharaoh and his entourage, changing their minds about letting the Hebrews go from their slavery in Egypt, decided to pursue them. The Hebrews' passage through the Red Sea is the most dramatic part of the Exodus. The Israelites were on the brink of extermination, the wind parted the waters, they went through safely, and the Egyptians were drowned. Although this passage sees the destruction of the Egyptian army as vindicating Yahweh's struggle over Pharaoh, Jewish tradition recognizes the ambiguity in freedom won by a military victory: the enemy is also a child of God. An ancient rabbinical legend recounts how the angels of God broke out into cheers when they saw the Egyptians drowning, but they were immediately silenced by God, who said, "My creatures are drowning, and you're singing songs of joy?"

The destruction of the Egyptian army marked a new stage in the life of Israel. From here on, the Hebrews were no longer a people fleeing as refugees; they were confronted with the burden of freedom.

God was at work through all the secondary causes that filled the Exodus event. Creation was made over anew, for the miracles of the Exodus were like a repetition of the first creation. The cloud overshadowed the camp (Ex 14:19f.), just as the darkness had covered the waters at creation (Gn 1:2); dry land emerged out of the Red Sea (Ex 14:21f.) as it had from the primeval waters (Gn 1:9f.); and from the land came vegetation ("grassy plain," v. 7; Gn 1:11-13). The passage concludes with a song of praise and thanks to God sung by Moses and the Israelites.

The flight of this small group of Hebrews from the yoke of Egypt is the core of what we celebrate tonight. The Exodus is Israel's coming through the waters of chaos into life. The Exodus is the ground of the covenant with God. We celebrate the new Exodus, the new creation, the new covenant. The history from Exodus back through creation and from Exodus forward culminates in the good news of Jesus which St. Paul talks about in this evening's portion of his Letter to the Romans.

Christians, in a world of sin, must live out their baptism. In Paul's time, baptism was by total immersion. This symbolized dying to sin so as to rise and live the new life that Christ intended: a life of liberation from the power of sin and death. This involves incorporation into Christ and into his body, the Church. Thus a new creation takes place whereby we begin the lifelong process of dying to sin and becoming alive for God with the new life of the gospel.

We become fully alive through generous giving of ourselves. That doesn't mean only pulling out a checkbook and writing some figures for charity, important as that is to many worthy causes. It's more important to give of our *self* to people: in the way we speak about them, in the way we forgive their failings, in the way we encourage them, in the way we show them hospitality, and even in the way we think about them.

It's divine generosity that's the source of the gift of grace. Grace is bestowed at baptism and makes the baptized person capable of effectively responding to the dictates of his or her conscience concerning faith and life. This renewal is the prelude to the Christian's bodily resurrection and admission to eternal life. If we have died with Christ we shall also rise with him and pass from death to life.

Matthew 28:1-10 (Cycle A)

St. Matthew presents the resurrection as a great intervention of God inaugurating a new order. The empty tomb was surrounded by miraculous phenomena: a great earthquake, an angel arriving with the appearance of lightning and snow-white clothing, guards paralyzed with fear, the angel delivering a message and rolling back the stone that covered the Lord's tomb, the risen Lord greeting the women.

Of importance in proving Jesus' resurrection was the empty tomb. It was the first day of the Christian week when the women came to it. It was Jewish custom to visit the tomb of their beloved departed for at least three days after burial. Jesus' friends couldn't visit on the Sabbath, because that would be breaking the Law of Moses, so by Sunday the women's overpowering love for Jesus could wait no longer: Early in the morning, when it was still dark, they went to the tomb. The women alone had remained faithful to the end, and now they became apostles to the twelve Apostles.

In retrospect, one might say that some First Testament passages had suggested the resurrection (for example, Ps 16:10; Hos

6:2; Jon 1:17; 2:1), and that the Apostles should have understood. But, while it may be true that life may be fully understood only when viewed backwards, it must be lived forwards. The Apostles didn't yet understand the Scripture about Jesus rising from the dead; this phenomenon was unique in all the history of the world.

Yet the overpowering wonder of this mystery wasn't intended to paralyze everyone to the point of immobility, nor to stun people beyond words. The disciples weren't told by the women to build a shrine around the Holy Sepulchre and make it an object of world pilgrimage. They were told to go up north to Galilee, where they would see Jesus and receive further instruction about preaching his message to the world. Matthew tells us later (v. 16) that they did just that.

Mark 16:1-8 (Cycle B)

St. Mark's gospel, the first to be written, was the briefest. He ended his gospel with these eight verses which give us a small picture of the resurrection. The women discovered that Jesus' tombstone had been rolled back, a young man in white told them that Jesus had indeed risen, and they fled trembling, bewildered, and afraid.

Dissatisfied with such an abrupt ending, a later author put together a synopsis of Easter appearances from the other gospels. For example, Jesus' appearance to Mary Magdalene (v. 9) is more fully described in Sts. Matthew (Ch. 28), Luke (Ch. 24), and John (Ch. 20). Jesus' closing command to the disciples to proclaim the good news (v. 15) echoes his mandate in the last chapter of the other gospels.

None of the evangelists intended to mention all the women there; each followed his own information without seeking to be in harmony with the others. But it will be observed that Mary of Magdala always heads the list. She must have been the most eager of the group. The women knew nothing of the fact that the tomb was sealed and a guard set there.

The burial on Friday evening had been so hasty that there had been no time to anoint Jesus. The Sabbath had ended at sunset on Saturday evening, and with it the prescribed Passover rest. The women had probably prepared the spices already on Friday. The stricken guards had recovered their senses and fled to the city to report.

The women had gone to the tomb at the bidding of their generous hearts, only realizing the difficulty that lay before them as they went along. They knew nothing about the guards. How were they to get into the tomb to anoint the body of Jesus? They had no hopes of finding a willing man (with a crowbar) to roll away the tombstone at that early hour. Great was their joy at seeing the stone already rolled back. It was hardly surprising that they — especially Mary Magdalene — set out to come to the sepulchre without giving a thought to the stone which closed it, for all their thoughts were concentrated on Jesus alone.

Luke 24:1-12 (Cycle C)

St. Luke presents the resurrection as the pivot of salvation. It brings to completion the ancient prophecies appropriated by Jesus. It's at the same time the beginning of the mission of the Church. The women who came to minister to the dead were called instead to be apostles of life.

Among the women Luke mentions, in addition to Mary Magdalene and Mary the mother of James, an unexpected mention is one Joanna (v. 10). She was the wife of Chuza, Herod's steward. While Jesus was journeying through towns and villages, preaching and proclaiming the good news of the kingdom of God, with him, in addition to the Twelve, were certain women who tended to him. Luke there mentions (cf. Lk 8:3) Joanna as being among them. Judging from Joanna's husband's office, she was an affluent and influential woman.

The women told their experience of the empty tomb to the Apostles, who thought it nonsense (v. 11), and didn't believe them. Peter ran to the tomb (v. 12) to see for himself (which was true to his nature). Stooping down, he saw the linen cloths laid there. And he went away wondering to himself at what had come to pass. Had the body been stolen, the wrappings would not have been removed. Now at last it was beginning to dawn on Peter and the others that this was the predicted fulfillment of the Messiah's final consecration (Is 53:11).

Conclusions

When we say or sing, "Jesus Christ is risen today," we don't mean only "Jesus Christ was risen once upon a time." We mean that the risen Christ is all around us, in the eyes and faces of those sitting beside us, in the bread and wine of the altar, in the newly baptized, in ourselves, in the people we meet all the time. He walks the earth today — teaching, healing, touching, suffering, dying, and rising. Seek him, address him, love him in every person by serving their needs. If we go seeking the risen Jesus with faith and hope and love we will find him. Then truly not only is Christ risen but we, too, are already living a risen life by his power and grace.

We should be able to update this collage of Jesus' resurrection by recalling the times the risen Jesus has come to us. We can begin with remembering his coming in the word and the sacrament of our Eucharistic celebrations. This is where the good news is proclaimed and experienced every day. It's all a cause for joy.

Sadness debilitates us. It's like heavy clay accumulating on our boots when we walk in the rain: it makes each step more difficult. But when we're happy, we're a stimulus and an encouragement for ourselves and others, carefree and light in the sunshine. To be happy is a form of giving thanks to God for the innumerable gifts He gives us.

Our joy brings others to God. Joy is frequently the best example of charity for those around us. Many people find the road to God in the cordial, smiling conduct of a good Christian. The first Christians' lives were attractive because of the peace and joy with which they did the commonplace things of ordinary life.

We take this serene, kindly joy to our homes and our work place and our social relations. God wants the home where we live and the places where we work and congregate to be bright and cheerful, never dark and unhappy. Supernatural life leads us to practicing those virtues (generosity, cordiality, a spirit of service) to which joy is so intimately connected.